TOM SEAVER

Portrait of a Pitcher

TOM SEAVER

Portrait of a Pitcher

by MALKA DRUCKER
with TOM SEAVER

Introduction by Tom Seaver

Holiday House, New York

For . . .
IVAN AND MAX
and . . .
SARAH LYNN AND ANNE ELIZABETH

Copyright © 1978 by Malka Drucker and Tom Seaver
All rights reserved
Printed in the United States of America

Library of Congress Cataloging in Publication Data
Drucker, Malka.
    Tom Seaver.: portrait of a pitcher

    Includes index.
    SUMMARY: A biography of the only major league pitcher
to have 200 or more strikeouts in nine consecutive
seasons.
    1. Seaver, Tom, 1944-   —Juvenile literature.
2. Baseball players—United States—Biography—Juvenile
literature. [1. Seaver, Tom, 1944-   2. Baseball
players] I. Seaver, Tom, 1944-   joint author.
II. Title.
GV865.S4D78   796.357′092′4 [B] [92]   77–17519
ISBN 0–8234–0322–X

Contents

2014204

List of Photos

8 List of Photos

Introduction

To know and fully understand Tom Seaver, you have to understand the tremendous importance pitching has been in my life.

There are many times when someone will ask, "I don't want to bore you, but how did a pitcher like so-and-so hurt his arm?" I could spend hours responding to that kind of question. The answer contains all the elements of pitching that I like to talk about: training, style, mechanics, technique and discipline, all of which are part of my story.

To me, pitching is an art form, a physical art form. Great dancers of our time, like Edward Villella and Rudolf Nureyev, certainly are artists in their field. They are creative, physical artists. And great pitchers, those who have learned to understand and master the functions of their bodies, also are creative artists.

Pitching is not an art that leaves an end product like a great painting or a great piece of sculpture. Rather, the benefit is a visual experience for all the people who attend baseball games and are lucky enough to see an artist at work. There have been many people in my life

9

who have helped me develop an understanding of this beautiful art—many of them, and many of the events that have shaped my career, are in this book.

I've been very fortunate to have experienced many beautiful things in a relatively short period of time. However, my career has not been the result of luck, but rather of determination and hard work.

I've put in long, hard hours at my profession, but I love it and the work hasn't bothered me. Any person who finds something he really enjoys, something he really loves and works hard at to become the best he can be, can thank those people who have helped him along the way; but for the most part, he can thank himself for the results of his own efforts. Baseball has been that element in my life. To me it is a continuing educational process. After spending more than ten years in the major leagues, I'm still learning about pitching.

Baseball, and to be more exact, my pitching rotation, determines many phases of my life. It determines my diet, whether I'll eat steak or spaghetti. It determines the amount of sleep I'll try to get at night. It determines the amount of exercise I will get each day. And it involves sacrifices, such as being kept away from my family for almost half the year. But I love it and remain dedicated to the creative art of pitching.

I only hope you are fortunate enough to find something to love in your life the way I have grown to love pitching.

1 . . .
The Perfect Game

The California sun shone brightly, but in the early morning chill Tom Seaver blew on his hands to stay warm. He peered through the chain link fence at the baseball field, waiting impatiently for the North Fresno Rotary League tryouts to begin. He was one of a group of boys standing by the fence, but he hoped the coach noticed he had been the first one there. In his eight years, this day seemed more important than any he could remember.

Finally, the coach walked across the hard, dry field of the junior high school to let the boys through the gate. Tom eagerly sprinted over to the baseball diamond; he was ready to prove he belonged on the team.

After looking at all the boys carefully, the coach studied his clipboard. As he had feared, there were too many boys and some would have to be cut. The quickest way would be by age.

"I'm sorry, boys," he said, "but this year you have to be nine to play on the team." He paused for a moment and read the names of the boys who qualified. Tom crossed his fingers and hoped he would hear "George Thomas Seaver," his full name, but no such luck. "See the rest of you next year," he said, dismissing the younger players.

Tom stood on the field, unmoving, as he watched the coach gather the nine-year-olds together. His eyes stung with tears of anger and disappointment. Quickly, before anyone saw him crying, he raced off the field to get his bike and ride home.

As he rode along the wide quiet streets of Fresno, he sniffed back bitter tears. It wasn't fair. He knew he could play as well as any nine-year-old. He couldn't help having been born November 17, 1944, instead of 1943. He was sick of being too young—it was the story of his life.

Being the youngest of four children put him at a constant disadvantage. His older brother, Charles, at sixteen, and his sisters, Carol and Katie, outplayed him at everything. They understood he was smaller and were sympathetic about it, but Tom still hated always losing, no matter how fiercely he competed.

Charlie and Betty Seaver, Tom's parents, encouraged a healthy competition among their children. Warm and loving, they taught their children to strive to be the best at whatever they attempted. As a result, Tom's brother and his sisters excelled both in sports and school. With such a family, Tom had to distinguish himself as more than the family mascot.

Tom (age 5) between his father and mother with (from left to right) Charles, Jr., Katie, and Carol

By the time he reached home, Tom's usually clear, hazel eyes were red from crying. He dropped his bike in the garage and ran into the comfortable house he had always lived in.

"Mom?" Tom called, wandering in and out of rooms. From his voice his mother knew something was wrong and called out to him from her room. He ran to her and jumped on her bed, sobbing. His sturdy body shook as he tried to tell her what happened at the tryouts.

As Mrs. Seaver comforted him, she remembered when he wanted to play baseball so much one day that he invented imaginary teammates and argued with an imaginary umpire who called him out on a slide. Another time, when Tom was six and not yet allowed to cross the street by himself, he and his friend, Russ Scheidt, who lived across the street, discovered they could play catch if they threw the ball carefully to one another. Because the game would be over if the ball rolled into the street, they both became accurate throwers and catchers by the end of the day.

Tom had two reasons for wanting to be on the team. Besides obviously loving baseball, he wanted to be somebody in a family of fine athletes. In addition to his brother and sisters, his mother played golf and his father was one of the best amateur golfers in the state.

When Tom's family heard about his bad luck, they all tried to cheer him up by playing ball with him. As the days grew longer, Mr. Seaver began to play pepper with Tom every night after dinner. Mr. Seaver would bat and Tom would field. It soon became obvious to

Mr. Seaver that Tom was a natural athlete—he could catch, he could bat, and he could throw especially well. He encouraged Tom to take his baseball seriously and be the best player he could.

A year later Tom made the team. He came home proudly wearing his North Fresno Rotary League uniform bearing the number 13 and looking forward to playing under Coach Hal Bicknell.

By the time he was eleven, he played every position well and was also the best hitter. Besides his ability, his coach liked Tom's competitiveness and his striving for perfection. Even when the opposing team teased him when he was pitching and the coach saw tears rolling down Tom's face, Tom's will to win was so strong he just set his jaw and kept the balls fast and low.

The next spring Tom decided to become a pitcher. He could hit well—he hit ten home runs the year before—but pitching especially challenged him. He liked controlling the game from the mound. So he worked all spring on throwing strikes, getting the ball over the plate. He hated to walk a batter, because it seemed like a gift.

On a sunny Saturday in July, when the normal temperature in Fresno, California, is in the one hundreds, Tom's family had come to see Tom pitch. He was a little nervous before the game, but when he saw his parents sitting in the first row in back of centerfield with his dog, Little Bit, he relaxed. He wanted to show his family, his father especially, how well he could pitch.

He walked out to the mound, already sweating from

The 1954 North Fresno Rotary League team with Coach Hal Bicknell. Tom is second from left in front row. On his left is Russ Scheidt.

the high sun, and looked around. The small Little League field was filled with nervous parents and friends. Tom took a deep breath and threw his first pitch. Perfect. Exactly where he wanted it. The batter swung and missed. Tom reared back again and threw another strike. Then he outsmarted the batter again and struck him out.

When Tom returned to the dugout bench in the fifth inning, his heart was pounding. He hadn't given up a hit or a walk, and had a chance to pitch a perfect game. The very thought made his hands sweaty. But he controlled his nerves by concentrating on just one batter at a time, and by the sixth and last inning he was still hanging on. Everyone in the stands, even the opposing fans, was rooting for Tom to pitch a perfect game. He had faced seventeen batters and had struck out fourteen of them.

The last batter came up to the plate. Tom wiped his hands on his uniform again and threw a high ball. Ball one. Tom was so nervous now he wished the batter would just strike out on anything he threw. But the batter saw Tom was having trouble getting the ball over the plate and gambled on a walk.

The next ball was a strike, but the batter still didn't swing. Tom had worked the count up to 2–2 when he threw a perfect strike. The umpire missed it and called it a ball. Tom shook his head in disbelief but didn't say a word. He threw the next pitch and watched it sail by the batter's eyes. "Strike!" the umpire called. The umpire had made it up to him. The batter didn't know what had happened, but Tom had pitched the perfect game. He threw his cap in the air and ran over to his parents. It was the greatest day of his life.

Tom always wanted to be a big leaguer, but by the time he was thirteen, it was just a dream that couldn't happen. He wasn't a star anymore. He still pitched with fine control, but he had stopped growing as fast as his friends. The boys he overpowered with speed and control a year before were now taller and could hit his fastball easily. Day after day he'd throw baseballs against the chimney of his house, but he knew he wasn't going to be a star, no matter how hard he tried.

2 . . .
Growing Up

When Tom was a small boy, his mother read him *The Little Engine That Could,* a story about an engine that pulled a freight train up mountains, telling itself, "I think I can, I think I can . . ." His parents wanted him to believe, as they did, that any goal could be reached. At fourteen he learned that the goals would have to be realistic.

When he didn't make the varsity baseball team in high school he wasn't surprised. After all, he was only 5 feet, 6 inches tall and weighed 140 pounds. Dick Selma, a junior, was 6 feet tall and already had major league scouts looking at his blazing fastball when he pitched varsity games. Tom didn't belong on that team.

What was interesting, though, was that Tom still won most of his games for the junior varsity. Years later when Dick Selma was pitching for the New York Mets, he explained Tom's success. "Tom was a heck of a pitcher, as contrasted to a thrower, even when he was on the JV's," he said. "He knew how to set up hitters, and him just in high school—I'm still learning now." What Selma didn't know was the hours Tom worked at compensating for his size.

His senior year Tom made the varsity team and perfected his technique. His coach, Fred Bartels, called Tom a "junkball pitcher" because Tom had so many weird pitches. But Bartels had to admit that Tom was good at setting up a batter and then luring him to swing at "out pitches." He threw slow curves, knuckleballs, change-of-pace pitches, anything to confuse the batter. Deadly serious, he concentrated hard on each pitch and rarely walked anyone. He learned that hitters took advantage of his mistakes, so he strove harder and made fewer of them.

Bartels always was amazed when he saw Tom's seriousness and concentration on the mound, because it was a different Tom Seaver he knew on the other side of the foul line. Tom was "the most happy-go-lucky guy you ever saw," he recalled. The team depended on Tom to ease the tension before a game, and Tom readily obliged. At home he was stuck as kid brother, but here he was the leader of the team, and he loved it.

The varsity team, having finished first, traveled to Ontario, California, for the league playoffs. On the bus Bartels overheard the players talking about cards and gambling. "Sorry, boys, no card games on this trip," he said firmly. "Gambling causes bad feelings, and besides, if you sit in your room and gamble all day long you'll have a hard time seeing the baseball later."

When they got to Ontario, they went to dinner, and

after dinner Bartels heard the boys laughing, Tom's laughter rising above the others. Bartels turned around, and in the darkness could see little except that Tom and Dick Selma had something on their shoulders. Knowing Tom, he was suspicious, but decided to wait and see.

At the hotel Bartels went downstairs to sit in the lobby, and the boys disappeared upstairs. Suddenly, he heard the whole team, thirty-five to forty boys, yelling and screaming. He ran quickly to beat the hotel manager upstairs, and in the hall he saw the boys crowded in a circle. Peering over the crowd, Bartels found them gambling—but not with cards. Tom and Dick were racing mice, and the boys were betting on them. Cleverly, Tom had discovered if he blew on the mouse's bottom it would run faster, and he was cleaning the house. Bartels knew at once why Tom could pitch varsity baseball—he used his head. He couldn't throw the ball nearly as hard as Dick Selma, but with finesse he was able to win the same number of games.

In the fall Tom had wanted to play football, but his mother wouldn't let him because she was afraid he would get hurt. So he waited to play basketball and worked hard enough to make the all-city varsity team. The basketball season strengthened his legs, and the following spring he discovered the stronger his legs, the faster his pitches.

Tom felt most complete when he was part of anything athletic. A physical person, he found his mind most clear on a baseball diamond or basketball court.

He loved all sports, because as an athlete he felt sure of himself. His quick decisions on the field and his ready wit also won him friends, but off the field he remained shy and awkward. He still felt like a kid brother who wasn't quite big enough, smart enough, or important enough.

Except for sports, school offered him little. He squeaked by in his classes doing only what was required, and except for his athlete friends, he had no social life. Those who knew him slightly in high school remember Tom as quiet and unassuming.

When he wasn't in school or playing ball, he and his friend, Mike Podsakoff, spent their afternoons hanging out at Hal's barber shop or tearing apart Mike's '58 Chevy. If the car worked, they drove it everywhere—on roads or through the dense groves and orchards that marked Fresno as an agricultural capital. Most people in Fresno earned their living from the abundant figs and grapes, including Mr. Seaver.

Mr. Seaver, vice president of Bonner Packing Company, had plans for Tom's future. Tom would go to Fresno City College, major in business, and then join him at Bonner. He wanted a secure future for his son, but Tom felt otherwise. Although he wasn't sure what he wanted to do, he knew he didn't want to stay in Fresno.

His uncertain future clouded his senior year. At every game he pitched he watched the scouts and prayed one would talk to him. Wade Blasingame, Dick Ellsworth, Jim Maloney, and Dick Selma had all been drafted from Fresno. But even though he pitched well enough to win six out of eleven games, he was still too small at 5 feet, 9 inches, 160 pounds, to impress the scouts with his power.

His parents, never having considered a professional baseball career for Tom, were relieved that he wasn't picked, but Tom was crushed. All he wanted to do was to play baseball, but neither the colleges nor the big leagues wished to recruit him. He didn't know who he was and didn't know what to do. He felt lost and pressured at the same time, knowing his father was disappointed with his indecision.

He had to do something, though, because the army was interested in Tom's future, too. With the Vietnam war on, he certainly would be drafted if he wasn't in school. If he didn't decide soon, he'd find himself in the army for three years. So one morning he called Russ Scheidt, his old friend who was just as confused as Tom, and talked him into enlisting with him in the Marine Reserves for six months.

In the meantime, Tom had a six-month wait before the Marines would call him. At his father's urging, he went to work at Bonner Packing Company. His father got him the job, but Tom soon found it was hardly an executive position.

It was still dark when he arrived at work and walked over to the foreman for his instructions. "See those sweat boxes over there?" the foreman asked, pointing his finger. Tom saw boxes, piled six feet high and almost four feet square, near the wall. "Pull them onto the platform for washing," the foreman ordered.

Tom grabbed one end of the box and tried to lift it. As he grunted with effort, beads of perspiration broke across his forehead. Now he knew why they were called sweat boxes. After he had lifted four of them, he pulled off the fifth box and saw something move. He was about to ask one of the men about it, when a pair of snake eyes stared at him. He nearly dropped the box. The other men laughed and told him that was nothing compared to the rats that often jumped out of them.

He hated the job so much he almost looked forward to the Marines. At night he played American Legion baseball to take his mind off work. He didn't play, though, when the extraordinary Dodger left-hander, Sandy Koufax, was pitching in Los Angeles. Tom, sitting high in the bleachers of Dodger Stadium, marveled at the man and his skill. "He had an artistic style," Tom would say later. "He used every part of his body in pitching. His mechanics were what I watched. He was so smooth."

Even when Koufax wasn't great, Tom admired him. One day Tom watched him get knocked out in the first inning, one of the few times that ever happened. Walt Alston came out to replace him, and Koufax just walked off gracefully. Tom ached to be that man on the mound with so much style and skill, but he buried the wish. He just couldn't—no matter how hard he tried—throw the ball fast enough anymore to dream of playing major league baseball.

In the Marines

The Marines unwittingly helped decide Tom's future. Two weeks of mindless discipline and incredible punishments convinced him he wanted to go to college. He and Russ laughed about the drill instructor kicking Tom for talking during dinner, but boot camp proved to be torture.

Besides the constant orders he endured, Tom suddenly was growing and his body kept getting in the way. He banged his left knee so many times it became swollen and infected. Frantic that he might have to spend extra time in the Marines if he was incapacitated by it, one night he secretly took his pen knife and cut his knee open to drain it. Seconds afterwards, he worried he might have done permanent damage to his leg, but it was too late. Luckily it healed, and he was able to leave the Marines on time. At the end of the six months he had stretched to a powerful 6 feet, 1 inch, and weighed 198 pounds.

3 . . .
Tom Trojan

When he got home he was bursting with plans. Now he knew what he wanted to do—he would go to Fresno City College for one year and then, hopefully, win a baseball scholarship to the University of Southern California. His parents, however, didn't share his enthusiasm. They wanted him at home, not at U.S.C., and Tom's father took pride in sending his children to college. He didn't want Tom to depend upon a scholarship for his education.

But Tom had become more independent, and although he loved his parents, it was time to cut the strings. If his parents paid for his education, he would still be listening to good-intentioned advice he no longer wanted.

Len Bourdet, coach at Fresno City College, knew about Tom Seaver from his friend, Fred Bartels. When Tom told Bourdet about his plans for U.S.C., he was surprised. Bartels had told him Tom worked hard but wasn't nearly as talented as Dick Selma. "Well, let's see what you can do, Tom," he said, doubtfully.

Tom stood on the mound, nervous, but also curious. He knew he was much stronger with his new size but wasn't sure if he could pitch the same way. Maybe he'd lost his control.

Frowning with concentration, he looked down, raised his knee and fired the ball. Wham! The catcher, unprepared for such speed, dropped the ball and shook his stinging hand. Tom grinned, surprised. He had never thrown a ball that fast in his life. He whipped another sailing fastball home just to be sure the first wasn't pure luck.

Goodbye, junkballs—Tom had a fastball that commanded respect. Bartels, who had come to the practice, shook his head in disbelief. He didn't know this new, powerful Tom Seaver.

As Tom sat in the hot June sun, drinking beer with his baseball buddies after his last final exam, his mood was reflective. He was pleased with his baseball record —he had won his last eleven games for Fresno City. U.S.C. coach Rod Dedeaux had offered him a scholarship if he played well for the Alaska Goldpanners that summer. He was thinking about Alaska when Mike Podsakoff interrupted his thoughts.

Mike pointed to a pretty girl crossing the far side of the field and reminded Tom that she was Nancy McIntyre, the girl he'd had his eye on all year. This was his last chance to meet her.

Even though Tom had matured into a handsome young man, he still thought of himself as ungainly. Shy around girls, this girl Nancy made him uneasy. She was a cheerleader, popular, and usually surrounded by boys. Today, though, she was alone.

The heat, the beer and the relief of finals being over gave him courage, and before he thought twice, he sprinted across the field. Because he didn't know what to say when he got there, he simply tackled her and knocked her to the ground.

Gasping for breath, Nancy looked up in shock and saw something dark hovering over her. It was Tom grinning ridiculously. Then he picked her up, dumped her into the back seat of his car, and took her home. Despite his shyness, he had figured out a way to meet Nancy. Before he left for Alaska, they had become good friends.

The Alaska Goldpanners gave Tom the chance to test himself against hard competition. Only nineteen outstanding college prospects were picked each summer to play against the best college, military, and international amateur teams. Rod Dedeaux chose Tom to see how he would compare with the other players before he'd make him a U.S.C. Trojan. It was a fantastic opportunity, but as always, Tom had to prove himself before he was accepted.

Red Boucher, coach of the Goldpanners, was waiting for Tom when the plane landed in Fairbanks. "We're playing a game right now," he said quickly, "and we may need you. I brought a uniform with me. You can put it on at the field."

Tom had no time to be nervous. Boucher rushed him

to the ballpark and showed him the bullpen. After a few minutes, Boucher waved him in to pitch the sixth inning.

He walked slowly to the pitching mound, taking in the crowd and the charm of the old-fashioned field. Then he introduced himself to the catcher and threw his first pitch, a smoking fastball the batter missed. Tom relaxed and finished the game, saving a victory for his new team of all-stars. He may have been a starter in Fresno, but on this team he felt honored to pitch relief.

He became friends with Goldpanner outfielder, Rick Monday, and on their days off they went exploring Alaska for its legendary fishing spots. Usually, all they found were mosquitoes, but they always had a great time talking baseball.

Red Boucher liked Tom's speed and his ability to outwit the batter, but he saw that Tom was affected too much by the crowd or the other team. He needed more confidence in himself. "It's an emotional game," he reminded Tom. "To be successful you must think you're successful."

Tom's confidence grew with each strikeout and victory. When Red chose him to go to the National Baseball Congress tournament in Wichita, Tom felt even more sure of himself.

His confidence was cut short when he was brought in to hold the Wichita Glassmen with the bases loaded. The Goldpanners led 3–2, but Tom walked in two runs before the inning was through. As he struggled for

Rod Dedeaux

control, the Goldpanners rallied in the ninth inning by loading the bases with two out. Tom was up next. Boucher looked over to Tom and wondered if he should take him out for a pinch hitter, but Tom was already kneeling determinedly in the on-deck circle, and the expression on his face convinced Boucher to let him hit.

Tom swung hard at the second pitch and watched amazed as it soared 450 feet. The pitcher had hit the winning grand slam home run! The crowd roared as Tom rounded the bases. His new muscles had helped his bat as well as his fastball.

After the game, Boucher told reporters, "We have a lot of players who can throw the ball harder than Tom. He's no Sandy Koufax, and his curve and slider aren't much better than average by college standards. But his greatest asset is his tremendous will to win."

This characteristic, as well as Tom's good performance over the summer, convinced Dedeaux to give him the scholarship. Thrilled as he was to be going to U.S.C., Tom had no illusions about being a major league player. If he could pitch well enough to keep his scholarship, he'd be happy.

In the fall of 1964 he enrolled as a predentistry major and joined the Sigma Chi fraternity at U.S.C. At first he loved being at a big university in a big city, but fraternity life became phony and silly to Tom, who was older and more mature than his fraternity brothers. So he and Justin Dedeaux, Rod's son, moved into their own apartment near the campus.

Tom also missed Nancy. When he had been in Alaska he hadn't thought much about her, but at U.S.C. he found himself bored with most of the girls there. "All they're interested in is clothes and parties," he told Nancy. Compared to them, Nancy was down-to-earth.

By spring, Tom's interests completely turned to baseball, and all his efforts were toward getting into shape. Justin was amazed at Tom's dedication and drive. He worked as though he were the star pitcher of the Trojan baseball team. In fact, he struggled to be a starting pitcher. He lifted weights, exercised, and ran all the time. Even when he went to the beach with his friends, he did his running.

Jerry Merz, a physical education major at U.S.C.,

suggested Tom lift weights to increase his strength, and by the spring of 1965 his fastball had definitely improved.

As the number three pitcher, Tom had to fight to start for U.S.C., but by the end of the year he had won ten and lost only two games. Still he didn't think he could play professional baseball, until the Trojans played the Trojan alumni who had become big leaguers. The U.S.C. baseball team was renowned for the many fine baseball players it sent to the major leagues every year.

Tom pitched the first inning and the first batter was Ron Fairly, then the ace Dodger first baseman. When Fairly returned Tom's slider with a weak pop-up, Tom blinked. He had gotten a major league player out. Wow, maybe I can play major league ball, maybe I won't be a dentist, Tom thought joyfully. "Pretty good pitch, kid," Fairly shouted, and Tom went through the rest of the inning in a dream world.

When he returned in the fall of 1965, Tom noticed there were a lot of big league scouts watching him. He tried not to care and reminded himself there were always scouts at U.S.C. games. But this year was different. He could see it and feel it all around him. His pitches were special and everyone sensed the change. He was drawing closer to the perfection he dreamed about.

His teammates noticed Tom's improvement the second year, but more than that, they were impressed by his new confidence. His concentration and fortitude infected them when they played behind him, and invariably they played better when he was pitching. There was no question he was the team leader.

After years of hard work and disappointment, the ugly duckling finally had turned into a swan. All he needed now was a fantastic bonus to live happily ever after. It came soon enough—$50,000 from the Atlanta Braves—but the ending wasn't going to be a happy one.

4 . . .
Tom Terrific
Meets the Amazing Mets

Tom stood in his parents' house, smiling and accepting congratulations from the friends, relatives and well-wishers who had come to say goodbye and wish him luck. He loved being the guest of honor at his farewell barbecue—he had waited for this Sunday a long time.

Russ Scheidt, his old friend, put an arm around Tom and said, "Say hello to Henry Aaron for me." Although there was no envy in his voice, Tom heard the wistfulness. Russ would have given anything to be going to the Atlanta training camp, too.

At first Tom's parents were disappointed he was leaving school to become a ballplayer, but soon his excitement overcame their objections. If he wanted to be the best pitcher he could possibly be, how could they protest? He had learned their lesson well, and now they shared his high hopes.

The phone rang and Tom excused himself to answer it. After a few moments, he came back into the living room, his face pale. His mother looked at him and wondered what was wrong. "The contract's void," he said, flatly. "The Braves broke the college rule of drafting me after the season began." U.S.C. had already played two games, even though Tom hadn't pitched in those games. The party went on, with most of the people not knowing the bad news. Tom soon recovered his composure when his father reminded him he could still play another year for U.S.C.

A week later Rod Dedeaux gave Tom the worst news. The NCAA ruled Tom couldn't play for U.S.C. that year either, because he had signed a professional contract. Angry and baffled, Tom turned to his parents for help. His father sent a letter to the baseball commissioner, William Eckert, requesting an explanation. He argued that his son would have to be "a Philadelphia lawyer to know what he could or could not do." The reply to his letter was more confusing than the contract Tom had signed.

Tom decided to call Commissioner Eckert himself to explain his dilemma. The Commissioner's assistant, Lee MacPhail, listened to Tom's plea for some solution. Two days later Commissioner Eckert himself called back to tell Tom that any interested team, except Atlanta, could draft him if they matched the Braves' offer.

He was relieved with the solution but worried no other club would make a bid. His confidence bounced up and down for a month, until the Commissioner called him back to announce three teams were interested—the Cleveland Indians, the Philadelphia Phillies, and the New York Mets. A lottery with the three clubs would be held one week later, April 2nd, in New York.

All the teams were thousands of miles from Fresno, far from Nancy. Tom wondered why the Dodgers weren't interested. Two years before, Dodger scout Red Adams had offered him $2,000, but he had turned it down in hopes of winning a U.S.C. scholarship. Actually they were interested, but Buzzy Bavasi, their general manager, was so immersed in contract disputes with his star pitchers, Sandy Koufax and Don Drysdale, that he forgot to send the Commissioner the telegram to include the Dodgers in the lottery.

He weighed the three eastern teams carefully to decide which would be best for him. Cleveland, with stars like Sam McDowell and Sonny Siebert, and the well-established Phillies, offered Tom prestige. But he wanted to be on a team that desperately needed a good pitcher and would advance him quickly. The Mets, a legend for their incompetence, could certainly use him.

April 2nd dragged interminably. Finally, late in the afternoon the phone rang. Tom picked it up in the den and signaled to his father to pick it up in the kitchen. It was Lee McPhail. "The three teams have put their names in the hat," he told Tom. A pause. "Now the Commissioner is reaching into the hat and taking out one slip and handing it to me." Tom took a deep breath and crossed his fingers. "And the team is," MacPhail read, "the New York Mets." A smile broke across Tom's face.

"Mom," he shouted. "Guess what?"

"Not the Mets!" she said, putting her hands over her face in mock horror. He nodded happily.

Now it was all settled. He was to report to the Met minor league camp in Homestead, Florida, a few days later, but first he bought Nancy an engagement ring with part of his bonus money.

Then he flew to Florida, wondering if he could believe what Nelson Burbrink, the Met scout, told Tom when he signed his contract. He had assured Tom that he would be playing AA or AAA baseball that spring. Tom was thrilled, because the best he had hoped for was to finish in AA ball by the end of the season.

Homestead, Florida, looked as ugly as a Marine boot camp, but he didn't care—he was happy just to be there. Minor league camps, with little money for frills, were often run-down places.

He walked into the locker room and changed into his uniform for his first day of practice. The other players wore blue, long-sleeved shirts under their uniforms, but Tom only had his bright maroon sweat shirt from U.S.C. He looked out of place and was embarrassed.

Writers and front office people surrounded him, asking him questions, giving advice. The other players watched Tom warily. They had heard about this college guy who had been offered a lot of money and a AAA position. Some of them had sweated on A and AA teams for five years before they made it to AAA. When they saw this clean-cut Californian in his college uniform, they expected a showoff.

Tom sensed the competitive, almost hostile atmosphere and understood it. Each man's performance threatened another man's job. They played musical chairs in the minor leagues, five men racing for one position.

Bud Harrelson, Tom's first and best friend on the Mets, remembered, "We were getting ready for the first batting practice and Tom was supposed to throw. I say to myself, This kid's gonna throw the ball through the wall. He's not gonna let anybody hit it.

"He walked out there to the mound, and all he did is lay the ball right in there and everybody was knocking the heck out of it. Right away I thought, I like that guy. He's not trying to impress anybody. He's getting loose; he doesn't care; his ego doesn't need to strike out the team. This kid's got some class!" Two years later Bud asked Tom if he wanted to room with him, an arrangement that lasted eight years.

Bud and Tom were soon sent up to the Triple-A Jacksonville Suns in Jacksonville, Florida. Solly Hemus, the manager, was impressed immediately with Tom's poise. "Tom Seaver is the best pitching prospect the Mets have ever signed," Hemus told writers at the time. The writers, having heard this claim every spring since the Met's beginning in 1962, weren't impressed.

The New York press had covered the worst players on the worst team in baseball for four years. When Tom signed with them, he knew the Mets were second-rate, but he didn't know their incompetence was newsworthy. The writers soon taught him the outrageous truth. The Mets had set every negative statistic imaginable: longest losing streak, most errors, worst E.R.A. for pitchers. They were unquestionably the worst baseball team in history. But they were loveable losers largely because of these writers who found the Mets so funny.

They couldn't write of heroic players, so they wrote of the outfield of Gus Bell, Richie Ashburn, and Frank Thomas that was prolific enough to have fathered twenty children. They had funny players like Marv Throneberry, who the fans called Marvelous Marv. He booted most grounders and waddled under pop flies only to drop them. Once, having slammed a long ball for a triple, he forgot to touch first and second before reaching third. The fans loved the bumbling, and expressed their love with banners. "Help" or "Pray" were common messages.

Tom, however, wasn't amused or frightened by these stories. In fact, he pitched exceptionally well and looked like the "prospect" everyone expected him to be. In his first game during a series against the Rochester Red Wings, he struck out nine, and allowed only six hits and two earned runs in 8⅓ innings. In his next appearance he was even better. He pitched a 6–0 shutout against the Buffalo Bisons and struck out eleven. One of the Bisons who went down swinging just shook his head and said, "That fastball just exploded when it reached the plate."

Besides the blazing fastball, Tom's pitches always surprised the batter, because his windup never gave a clue. Whatever the pitch, Tom went through the same fluid motion. His left leg high, ready to kick and stride, ball pressed to his chest, he waited a moment to pull himself together, mentally and physically, to put everything into the pitch, and then fired the ball to home plate. The batter never knew if it would be a fastball, curve, or slider.

There was no question Tom was a sensation but skeptical veterans of spring training—writers and coaches—had seen many "wonder boys" fade away in May, never to return to their former spring glory. Tom began to fade even sooner than that. In less than a

After his pro debut,
April 25, 1966

month his pitching, after three consecutive wins, fell off, and he lost four games in a row. Writers speculated about the reason, but Tom knew the cause of his slump.

He discovered that all players at Jacksonville shared two things—hope and loneliness. They hoped to make the big leagues soon, and they found the minor leagues a painfully long way home. Also, the fierce competition strained friendship that may have eased lonely feelings. At twenty-one, Tom was one of the older players, but after three weeks he felt the loneliness too, and it began to affect his game.

"I'm going crazy in my tiny room at the Roosevelt Hotel," he wrote Nancy. They were going to wait until September to be married, but he asked her if she would join him and marry him then. In the letter he enclosed a one-way ticket to Florida. On June 9, 1966, Nancy and Tom were married quietly in Jacksonville, and from that day on his promise as a pitcher returned.

By the end of the season, people once again talked of him as the season's "phenom." Hemus declared, "Tom has a 35-year-old head on a 21-year-old body. Usually, we get them the other way around." His fastballs blazed and his curves and sliders zigged and zagged perfectly to the consternation of batters. Finishing with a 12–12 record, Tom felt hopeful he would make the 1967 Met team.

As they drove back to California in their new convertible, Tom wanted to share his joy with Nancy but saw something was wrong. She sat stiffly, reading a magazine. He asked what was bothering her, and she

Wedding day, June 9, 1966

told him she was questioning their hasty marriage. She didn't like being a ballplayer's wife. Most of the time she was alone in Florida while Tom traveled with the team. Besides the loneliness, she had heard from other players' wives about the drinking and girls on the road. Tom winced at the tears in her eyes as she talked, but he was firm. "As much as we're going to be separated you're going to have to trust me. When you married me, I think you knew that I could be trusted." Nancy nodded, but they both knew baseball would strain their marriage. Tom's long road trips would keep them from getting to know one another.

Tom and Nancy took an apartment in Manhattan Beach, not far from U.S.C. Tom wanted to return to school in the offseason, not only because he had promised everybody he would finish college, but also because pitching had helped him realize how important an education was. "Being a successful pitcher is not just being able to throw the ball, but being able to weigh and make quick decisions," he would say later. "College refines that and has helped me to make the right decisions on the mound. More than ever before, now I know pitching is using your mind."

While he was in his public relations class one winter morning, the Mets called and told Nancy they wanted Tom to report to the Met training camp at St. Petersburg for the 1967 spring training. After that it took all his concentration to study, because his mind kept wandering to a fantasy. Wearing the Met uniform, he'd be on the mound at Shea Stadium and up would come Henry Aaron. Slugger against pitcher. Over and over Tom would strike Bad Henry out. Whenever Nancy caught him daydreaming at his desk, she would remind him that until February books came before baseball.

When Tom reached St. Petersburg, he kept his fantasy to himself, fortunately. When the New York sportswriters started to hear about this guy Seaver and all the promise he had shown the previous spring, they laughed loudly again. They didn't know much about Tom except for his fair 12–12 record at Jacksonville, but they were sure of one thing. If he was good, he didn't belong on the Mets.

The writers had already begun the 1967 spring training with a funny story about a new center fielder, Don Bosch. The Met front office had touted Bosch as the hope of the Mets, a new Mickey Mantle. When Maury Allen, the *New York Post* writer, first saw him, he bit his lip to stop laughing and ran to his typewriter. The "sensation" was 5 feet, 7 inches, 27 years old, neurotic, and had gray hair. He belonged to the Met legend.

Tom, however, set out to prove he wasn't part of the Met legend. The comic atmosphere at St. Petersburg overwhelmed him. After a defeat one afternoon, Tom looked around the locker room and didn't see anyone who cared they had lost. Some of the players were actually laughing over a fielding error. Even with his well-developed sense of humor, Tom found nothing funny about losing. He couldn't believe his eyes, because he had never played baseball with a team that expected to lose.

As a rookie, though, who had yet to throw a ball, he decided to keep his thoughts quiet until he proved himself. Instead, he would concentrate on his own game. If he showed his stuff, if he concentrated, he stood a good chance of being one of the ten pitchers to travel north with the team. The unstable and weak pitching staff worked to a rookie's advantage.

His first test came in March, when he pitched against the Minnesota Twins. Orlando was terribly hot that day, 90 degrees, but Fresno had prepared Tom for the heat.

He came into the game in the fourth inning to face huge Harmon Killebrew, nicknamed Killer for his mighty bat. He would lead the American League in home runs (44) that year. The sparse crowd cheered Killebrew as he took a practice swing. The challenge electrified Tom. He wound up and watched his fastball sail in for a strike. I've got it, he told himself. Another strike. Smoke him now, he said to himself, and with a great stride whizzed the ball past Killer, who went down swinging. Tom walked to the dugout nonchalantly, but he was doing cartwheels inside.

He held the Twins to only two hits in his three innings, and Met Manager Wes Westrum decided, after Tom had successfully relieved a few games, that he was ready to be a starting pitcher. He pitched five strong innings against Kansas City, giving up only one run, and when he faced the 1966 World Series champs, the Baltimore Orioles, he pitched five scoreless innings.

He was pitching well enough to go to New York with the team, but he couldn't let up his intensity for a minute. He could only throw a ball one way—with every ounce of strength and concentration in him, and that effort required long hours off the field to condition himself. If the coach barked, "25 sit-ups," Tom did 50. If it rained and the players were excused from windsprints, Tom ran anyway. His legs, the key to his endurance, protected his arm from injury. Without strong legs that made his pitching motion smooth and complete, he would have to worry about arm strain. What other players did didn't concern him. He only knew he had to work very hard "to pitch the best Tom Seaver can do," he told a reporter who asked why he worked so hard. Panting from his windsprints, he

After a hard workout during spring training, 1967

added, "Pitching has always been hard work for me. I never had anything handed to me. At fourteen, I already knew my physical limitations. It appeared to be a burden then, but it obviously helped."

Despite his impressive record during spring training, the New York writers were only mildly interested in Tom. He was hard-working and competent, not the typical stuff Met stories were made of.

One afternoon Maury Allen strolled into a local bar in St. Petersburg to pick up some baseball gossip and heard to his amazement that Tom Seaver, rookie, might be the opening-day pitcher. Tom Seaver. The smooth-faced kid from California, who looked so young the players called him Spanky, was going to start.

All Allen could remember about Tom, besides his record, was that he was like most rookies—quiet, shy, anxious to please, and nervous about making it to the big leagues. The writers had been playing with Don Bosch too much to notice Tom. Allen decided to confirm the rumor with Westrum. He found him in the clubhouse and without wasting time asked the uneasy manager, "Are you thinking of starting Seaver on opening day?" Caught off guard, Westrum admitted he had been considering Tom, but was afraid writers like Allen would second-guess him if Tom was shelled in the first inning. They'd blame him for starting with a rookie. Later that day, Westrum called the writers together to announce he would start the season with Don Cardwell, a seasoned pitcher. "Seaver will start in the second game," he told them.

The writers still gave Westrum a hard time. "Who starts a rookie even the second game?" a writer challenged.

"I'll admit he doesn't have much experience," Westrum retorted, "but he gets people out."

5 . . .
"Seaver Is Hurting
the Met Image"–1967 Banner

Tom awoke early on April 12th, a cold gray day, and felt the dancing butterflies that would stay with him until that afternoon, when he would pitch his first major league game. He was always nervous before a game, but today was the worst he could remember. He nibbled at some bacon Nancy put in front of him, as he pictured each Pittsburgh Pirate batter before him. He'd studied the hitters until he had memorized each style and stance. After breakfast he paced restlessly around their small apartment in Queens near Shea Stadium, staring at the wallpaper patterns. Finally, he went to get a haircut and then drove out to Shea.

The horeshoe-shaped, cold, concrete stadium did little to relax Tom, but inside the clubhouse Bud Harrelson and the other Mets helped him prepare mentally for the game. A spasm of nervousness recurred when he walked through the tunnel to the field and was struck by the noise and sight of 20,000 people in the stands.

49

Tom with his father at Shea

But once he got to the mound and threw his warmup pitches, he began to relax. He saw the ball skim the corners of the plate and knew he had control and speed. For five innings he pitched well, with the score tied 2–2. In the top of the sixth inning he felt his legs tiring, because he hadn't pitched more than five consecutive innings all spring. With great effort, he wound up and threw a weak fastball. The hitter smashed it for a base hit. From the corner of his eye, Tom saw Wes Westrum walking to the mound to take him out. He had run out of gas. The Mets won the game 3–2, but it was relief pitcher, Chuck Estrada, who earned the victory.

Tom pitched the following Thursday against the Chicago Cubs at Shea. He was determined to stay in longer for that game, even though he would be facing hitters like Ernie Banks, Ron Santo, and Billy Williams. The Mets scored three runs off the Cubs, and Tom was holding them to one run, but in the eighth inning he felt himself tiring. He took a deep breath, but only threw with half his normal drive. Glenn Beckert took advantage of the slow pitch and slammed it deep into center field. It would have been a triple, but Tommy Davis stopped the ball with a heroic leap.

Ken Boyer, the third baseman, walked over to Tom after the play and asked Tom how he felt. He wanted to say "strong," but he wanted the victory more. "Pooped," he said. Westrum brought in Don Shaw to finish the game. As Tom walked off the field, the fans loudly applauded the rookie pitcher. He had struck

The rookie with his parents

out five, allowed eight hits, and given up only one run. For New York fans, who had long watched the agony of the Mets, his performance was especially welcome.

Tom went into the clubhouse and quickly clicked on his radio to hear the rest of the game. If Shaw could hold the Cubs, it would be Tom's first major league victory. The Mets helped by scoring three runs in the bottom of the eighth inning, and Shaw finished the game easily. The team poured into the clubhouse, congratulating the rookie, and the writers circled around Tom with new interest. Once they had dismissed him as Spanky, but now they knew what Wes Westrum was talking about.

One of the writers asked Tom why he had left the game. When he told him he was tired, the writer was surprised. Most pitchers would rather collapse on the mound than admit fatigue.

After the game he and Nancy celebrated at their favorite Chinese restaurant with a big dinner. As usual, Tom was starving, because he was too keyed up to eat much before the game. Besides eating, Tom's sleep was changed, too. Two nights before he pitched, he slept eleven or twelve hours to make up for the wakefulness that followed the night after he pitched. While the rest of the city slept, Tom replayed every pitch, every swing, every play of the game.

Tom's mental notes on hitters became a real notebook filled with each pitch he threw to each batter. He remembered every crucial pitch, the ones that led to a key strike or a double play. After every game he jotted down what he'd done to each hitter—and what they had done to him.

Besides asking experienced teammates about batters, he also went to Ralph Kiner, the Met broadcaster, for advice. When Tom was ten, his father was playing in the Crosby Pro-Am golf tournament with Kiner, then a famous National League slugger. Mr. Seaver had asked him for an autograph for "my boy who one day will be in the big leagues." Now "the boy" was asking Kiner for advice, because Tom believed hitters knew hitters.

Tom learned more about the art of pitching every time he played, and as the season progressed his record showed it. By the end of June he had an 8–5 record, the best on the Mets. His confidence grew daily, and by the time the Mets flew to Atlanta to play the Braves, Tom couldn't wait. He would finally have the chance to face his boyhood hero, Henry Aaron. He had carefully studied Aaron for years and watched how other pitchers had faced this legendary player. Now he would have his chance.

Aaron strode to the plate and swung the bat a couple of times, then took his famous stance. Tom shot a glance to the plate and suddenly he was in a dream world, aware of only one game, the game between him and Aaron. It was a game the batter didn't know about.

Tom decided to pitch a sinking fastball, and sure enough, on the first pitch Aaron hit into a double play. Tom was so delighted with his strategy that two innings later he offered the same sinker, but this time Aaron swung hard and sent it sailing 400 feet into the stands. "Hitters remember pitches, too," Tom thought wryly. "I won't make that mistake again."

Despite his occasional mistakes, Tom won regularly enough to be chosen to play in the All-Star game in July. That Tom was the only Met to be chosen came as no surprise to New Yorkers. He had become the first National League celebrity in New York since Willie Mays. Tom's brother, Charles, who was working for the New York City Welfare Department, discovered his brother was a celebrity from one of his clients. Upon walking into a tenement kitchen, Charles saw Tom's picture neatly pasted on the refrigerator. "Hey, that's my brother," he said, surprised.

Grote, Seaver, Harrelson, and the satisfaction of victory after defeating the Reds 7–3, June 13, 1967

"Wow! He's some pitcher," the man informed him, and then recited Tom's entire pitching record.

Tom and Nancy flew to Anaheim, California, where the All-Star game would be played. Although he didn't expect to pitch in a game with pitchers like Don Drysdale and Juan Marichal in the lineup, his heart still jumped when he thought about just being part of the game.

He got to Anaheim Stadium around noon, four hours before game time, in the hope of meeting some of his heroes. He walked into the locker room, where St. Louis Cardinal Lou Brock was changing into his uniform. Brock looked up from tying his shoes, and seeing a round-faced boy in a seersucker jacket, assumed he was the clubhouse boy. "Can you get me a Coke, kid?" he asked.

Too embarrassed to say anything, Tom brought him the soda. "Hi," he said, putting out his hand. "I'm Tom Seaver of the New York Mets." Brock looked stunned for a moment as Tom enjoyed the misunderstanding and roared with laughter.

When Tom walked across the field to the bullpen, he blinked twice. Aaron, Clemente, Mays, Rose, Bench, Drysdale. He had paid to see these men play a year ago.

When Tony Perez hit a home run in the 15th inning and Walt Alston waved Tom in from the bullpen to protect the National League's narrow 2–1 lead, Tom looked over his shoulder to be sure it was he Alston wanted. His heart started to pound and his stomach became queasy; he felt like throwing up. Besides Nancy and his parents out there, he knew Sandy Koufax was watching the game. Koufax watching *him*.

As he left the bullpen, he tried to cover his nervousness with a little joke to Pete Rose at second base. "How about you pitching and me playing second base?" he shouted, as he jogged by.

Rose laughed, knowing what was going on inside Tom at that moment. "No," he said. "I'll stay where I am. You can do it."

Roberto Clemente, overhearing the conversation, gave Tom additional encouragement. "Go get 'em, Rookie," he yelled, smiling.

Tom stood on the mound, almost shaking. But with his first warmup pitch the nervousness faded and he began to enjoy the moment. When he finished warming up, he turned to check the outfield. "That's when I got my greatest thrill of the day," he said after the game. "Imagine turning round and seeing Clemente in right, Mays in center and Aaron in left and an infield of Cepeda, Alley, Rose and Perez."

He turned to face his first batter, Boston Red Sox Tony Conigliaro, a treacherous hitter. "Everyone here would be tough," Tom told himself. He wound up and threw a low fastball that was caught as an easy fly ball. The next man up was left-hander Carl Yastrzemski. He would win the American League's Most Valuable Player Award in 1967. Careful not to give the slugger anything to tie the game, Tom walked him. Bill Freehan, the next batter, hit a weak flyball to center, and Tom was one out away from saving the National League victory. He stepped off the mound for a moment, massaged the ball, and forced himself to concentrate.

He had never seen the next hitter, Ken Berry, but had been advised to pitch his fastball up and in. Carefully, he worked the count to two and two. Glancing at first, he threw the ball—up and in—and Berry went down swinging. Tom, immensely relieved by the out, began to walk off the field, when suddenly he felt this huge hand pound him on the back. It was Henry Aaron, grinning from ear to ear. Years later Tom would say, "Those two things with Henry are the two biggest thrills I've ever had—the experience of pitching against him for the first time, and then his congratulating me—terrific!"

Tom was pulled quickly into the exuberant spirits of the winning team in the clubhouse. They were yelling and jumping up and down over their victory. He was thrilled to be part of it but surprised at their enthusiasm. He had thought these guys, some of whom had been in several all-star games, wouldn't think it was so important. But he saw, on the contrary, that winning was always exciting and important to them. "That's why they're winners," he told Nancy as they flew home, "and that's what we need at the Mets." He was determined to inject the Mets with the same winning spirit he found among the best in baseball.

After one particularly inept game against Pittsburgh, Tom stood on a stool and announced to the team with

mock solemnity, "Gentlemen, after watching that performance, I would like to take this opportunity to
announce my retirement from the game of baseball."
It was funny, but the players got the message.

Although the sportswriters quickly spotted Tom's
ability, it took them awhile to discover his different
attitude. While everyone else was laughing about

With Henry Aaron

losses, Tom was a dedicated, serious, professional pitcher. The writers were surprised to see him upset when the Mets lost.

Also, some of them found Tom too good to be true. They mistrusted his regular features, his "Hollywood values," and even his "lovely wife." Privately, they thought of Tom as a plastic athlete married to a cheerleader. They respected his ability enough, however, to dub him Tom Terrific.

Tom's teammates, who knew him better than the writers, weren't deceived by his appearance—he got his uniform dirty and worked hard. Unofficially, he had become the clubhouse leader, because he played hard and gave them a chance to win. He was their stopper, a pitcher who could break losing streaks, and for Ed Kranepool, an original Met, Tom was a welcome change. The Mets finally had a pitcher who won more than he lost. They began calling him Supey, for super rookie.

Tom cared more about winning than what he was called. He wished everyone on the team shared his commitment and despised losing as much as he did. They had the ability to win, but they didn't seem to care. He did notice, though, that when he pitched the team played harder. They helped bring his record to 12 wins by August. He wished they would play hard all the time but didn't know what he could do about it.

On paper the Mets still looked like the same old losing team, but something happened one night that changed the attitude of the club. Tom was pitching against the Cubs with the Mets leading 1–0 with two out in the bottom of the ninth, when Ron Santo hit an easy grounder right to Bud Harrelson. The ball went through his legs for an error and cost the Mets a run.

In the tenth inning Tom singled, Cleon Jones moved him to second with a sacrifice fly, and Tom scored on a single. The Mets won 2–1. The first thing Tom saw when he walked into the clubhouse was Bud sitting alone, his head between hands, looking at his knees. He was suffering for giving up Tom's shutout and almost causing a defeat. In a strange way, Tom felt both sorry for Bud and glad to see how much the error meant to him. Later Tom said, "For the first time, maybe we realized that we had guys who cared deeply whether we achieved, that we even had pitchers who could hit occasionally and who wanted to win so desperately. Looking back, I think it was the first time in my experience with the Mets that we believed in each other, the first time I felt that I wasn't there to lose." By the end of the season Tom had broken most Met pitching records. With 16 wins he had already set a record for victories. He had completed 18 games, pitched 251 innings, struck out 170 batters, and walked only 78. He had given up four runs or less in eight of his thirteen losses. With another team he might have won twenty games.

Besides Met records, his 2.76 E.R.A. (earned run average)—the average number of runs a pitcher gives up in each nine innings pitched—ranked him among the top ten pitchers in the league.

Tom was back at U.S.C. when the Mets' publicity director called to congratulate him on being chosen Rookie of the Year—another first for the Mets and the first time a rookie-of-the-year had been chosen from a last-place team. Tom was thrilled with the award, but made his priorities clear to reporters. "It's nice, but I want to pitch on a Mets pennant winner, and I want to pitch the first game in the World Series. I want to change things ... the Mets have been a joke long enough. It's time to start winning, to change the attitude, to move ahead to better things. I don't want the Mets to be laughed at anymore," he finished.

Indeed, Tom Seaver had hurt the Met losing image.

6 . . .
"Break Up the Mets"–
1968 Banner

Hands in his hip pockets, Gil Hodges looked over the forty players in St. Petersburg carefully. The Mets had asked him for a miracle—to manage the '68 Mets out of last place. A low-keyed but powerful man, he had the respect of every Met facing him. His playing days as ace first baseman and slugger for the Brooklyn Dodgers had been over for ten years, but his tremendous size and strength reminded the team of his past glory. Many of the players had been hoping Hodges would be the man to replace Westrum when he resigned, because as manager of the last-place Washington Senators, he established a reputation for being tough, fair, and successful. In four years, he had taken the Senators into a race for first place.

Gil knew all about the Mets, because he had been an original Met in 1962. At 38, he was past his prime, but New York loved him so much they wanted him back. He suffered the ignominy of being with a team that lost 120 games and retired at the end of the season. But the Mets in 1968 were different. They were young, and with guidance they could improve.

After watching the team for five weeks, he weeded it to twenty-five and set to work immediately with the survivors, including Tom, Ed Kranepool, Jerry Grote, and Bud Harrelson. In addition, the team had bought Tommy Agee from the White Sox, a good center fielder who looked like a .300 hitter. Cleon Jones, Agee's buddy, was in left field and also showed promise as a hitter. With Ron Swoboda in right field, the Mets were hoping for an outfield of .300 hitters.

More than any other player, a pitcher depends upon the other players for his success. He depends upon a strong defense, and, naturally, he needs hitters. When Tom saw the improvement of this team over the previous year's, he couldn't wait to play.

In addition to the field, the pitching staff looked good. The past year Tom had been the pitching staff. He had won 16 games whereas the other pitchers had won 9 or less. This year Jerry Koosman, a farm boy from Minnesota who had learned to throw baseballs in a barn, threw hard and strong. Another pitcher, Nolan Ryan, from Texas, threw harder than Tom had ever seen anywhere.

Another newcomer to the training camp was Rube Walker, the pitching coach Gil Hodges had brought with him from Washington. An ex-catcher, Walker had seen enough pitchers to know this young pitching staff would be stronger with a five-day pitching rotation rather than a four-day rotation.

With Rube Walker

Over the winter in California, Tom had given much thought to his pitching. He wanted to cut down on his mistakes. Nineteen of them had become home runs the previous year. Tom didn't think more rest between pitching starts mattered. At first he didn't like the idea at all, because he had been successful with a four-day rotation and didn't want to interfere with what had worked before.

But once he got over the restlessness that annoyed him on the day he usually pitched, he found he was stronger with the new rotation. The entire pitching staff improved, and by the end of spring training, Met writers informed surprised New Yorkers that the young team had given up fewer runs than any other National League team.

Despite the optimism that abounded on the team, however, the other statistics remained dismal. The Mets won only 9 of their 27 games in spring training. Gil Hodges told writers, "All I want to do is show improvement over last season. We'll win at least 70 games this season."

After Tom's excellent first season, no one was surprised when he was chosen to pitch the first game of the 1968 season. The Mets traveled to San Francisco in April, determined to break their curse—they had never won an opening-day game. Despite legends like Willie Mays, Willie McCovey, and Juan Marichal, who was scheduled to pitch, the Mets felt they had a chance. Tom and the rest of the team had a new confidence in themselves and in their leadership.

Juan Marichal had an unbelievable record against the Mets of 19–1, but now the Mets had Tom Seaver. They played hard, and by the ninth inning, the Mets were three outs away from winning their first opening-day game. With the score 4–2, Willie Mays came up to bat. Tom looked at him from the mound. Not as intimidating as McCovey, but at 37 the man was still scary. Tom was tired; he hadn't pitched nine consecutive innings since the previous year. Still, maybe he could finish the inning quickly, and they could all run into the clubhouse to celebrate. . . . He released a fastball, but Mays was faster and drove it along the third base line for a single. Damn! McCovey was up next, and the fans were roaring. Settle down, Tom told himself. He wound up and threw the "money pitch," the pitch with everything he had left. It worked, because all McCovey could do was pop up a foul, and Kranepool caught it for the first out.

Hodges watched Tom anxiously, trying to decide if he should take him out. After the pitch to McCovey, Tom looked strong enough to finish. But a moment later, with Jim Ray Hart at bat, Tom threw a low pitch that Grote lost in the dirt. Mays, a man who knew how to take advantage of the moment, scooted to second. Tom turned to look at second base, exasperated. His next pitch to Hart hung in the air long enough for Hart to double and for Mays to score. Now the score was Mets 4, Giants 3.

Gil didn't need to see more. He replaced Tom with Danny Frisella and replaced Grote with J. C. Martin behind the plate. As much as Tom wished his legs hadn't tired, he was glad Frisella, an ex-Giant, had come in to relieve him. He should know how to pitch to them, Tom thought.

The end came so suddenly Tom couldn't believe it. Nate Oliver singled and Jesus Alou doubled to win the game 5–4. As Frisella said afterward, "Knowing how to do it isn't enough. You have to do it, too."

Bitterly disappointed, Tom sat in the locker room,

All-Star game, 1968

trying not to believe in the Met destiny. "I thought we had it," he said softly, to no one in particular. "I thought we had it."

Despite the loss, the Mets proved they were serious contenders who wanted to win. Their desire didn't help them off to a good start, however. The next game Tom pitched against the Astros remained scoreless for eleven innings. The game was finally ended in the bottom of the 11th inning with a Met error and the Astros won it 1–0.

In his four starts Tom had an E.R.A. of 1.59, but because the Mets weren't hitting, his record was an average 1–1. He had never pitched better in his life. His fastball zipped by batters so often that Pirate

Willie Stargell complained, "Hitting against Seaver is like trying to drink coffee with a fork." After ten starts, he had an E.R.A. of 1.91 but a 2–4 record.

After their slow start, the Mets began to win, and by July they were close to the .500 mark. Met fans were delighted to win one, lose one, but Tom wasn't satisfied by it. A bad pitch that caused a loss haunted him and interfered with his sleep.

The All-Star game at the Houston Astrodome took Tom's mind away from the season's frustrations. This year, besides Tom, Jerry Koosman and Jerry Grote would represent the Mets on the National League team. This year Tom was sure he would pitch, and the one batter he wanted to face was Mickey Mantle. Tom was pitching when Mantle was brought in to pinch-hit in the seventh inning. The fans stood up to cheer the aging Mantle. He had already announced he would retire at the end of the season.

All Stars Willie Mays and Tom

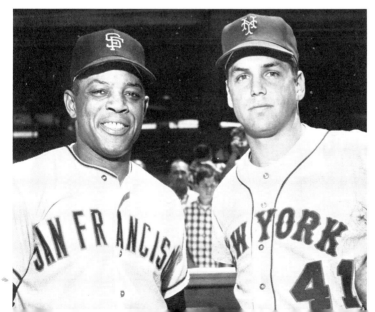

Tom had spoken to Grote about how to pitch to the great slugger. Mantle intimidated pitchers into pitching around him. Tom wanted nothing less than a strikeout. The classic confrontation between batter and pitcher began with a blazing fastball. Mantle swung too late. Two more smoking fastballs and Mantle went down swinging. Most of the fans were disappointed, but Tom had done his job.

By August the Mets were only three-and-a-half games out of second place, but they couldn't hold on. By the end of August they had fallen 24 games out of first place and had a 63–76 record. It looked as though they wouldn't even win the 70 games Hodges had hoped for.

The Mets finally won 73 games and landed in ninth place. Most of the credit went to the pitching staff, which had given up an average of three runs a game. Tom finished with a 16–12 record, but that was deceptive. His E.R.A. of 2.20 and 205 strikeouts revealed the team's chief problem, weak hitting. With an E.R.A. of 1.91 in eleven starts, Tom had only two wins, because the Mets supplied a stingy 19 runs in all those games. The pitchers needed more hits and Tom, sure the Mets had the power, was frustrated. He had hoped Gil could change the Met legend—fighting to stay out of the cellar was no fun.

Although Hodges only managed to move the club one place out of the cellar in 1968, he did teach the younger players what it meant to be major leaguers. Tom idolized Gil and listened carefully to his advice.

By watching him, he learned what it meant to be professional, and that the key was self-control.

But the self-control Gil Hodges practiced nearly killed him. One week before the season's end, the Mets were in Atlanta to play the Braves. Gil was hitting fungoes during batting practice when Tom saw him lean over suddenly and sit down. He thought Gil had dropped something. Then he noticed how gray and tired Gil looked.

After the game Tom asked, "Where's Gil?"

"The trainer took him to the hospital," the clubhouse boy answered. "He had a heart attack during the game."

After the season, Tom decided to volunteer his time to help crippled children. When he played baseball, he had no time for more than a handshake, but now he could visit hospitals and talk to these children. He felt grateful his success as a pitcher gave him something to offer. At times, though, he left weeping, almost ashamed of his health after seeing children who would never walk. But sometimes the ending was happy.

In Alaska, he visited a boy whose legs had been frozen from severe exposure. The doctors told Tom the boy had to try to walk or else they would have to amputate his legs. Tom told him, "If you get up and walk, I'll send you the baseball I used in winning my first major league game."

A short time later, Tom received a note from the

With Gil Hodges

doctor telling him the boy had walked and was well again. Tom gladly gave him the ball.

When they were at home, he and Nancy roamed New York City, enjoying its theaters, museums, and restaurants. They also spent time with his brother, Charles, who had left the Welfare Department to devote all his time to sculpting. Charles and Tom enjoyed discussing the difference between their work. Charles' effort, on the one hand, could be seen a century later without losing its beauty and drama. Tom's creation vanished in an instant. Still, Tom wouldn't trade places with anyone. Before 1968 ended, his thoughts turned to 1969. If we hit, if I win 20 . . . it will be our year. For Tom, spring training couldn't begin soon enough.

7 . . .
"Seaver Is Our Savior"–
1969 Banner

The bait plunked as Tom dropped his line into the water, breaking the quiet calm of the early spring evening in St. Petersburg. He turned to his fishing companions, Bud Harrelson and Jerry Grote, and said, "You know, we could win our division this year if we play up to our potential." No one disagreed, despite the 100-1 odds Las Vegas offered against the Mets winning the Eastern Division championship in 1969.

The National League, in expanding to twelve teams with the new Montreal Expos and the San Diego Padres, had been divided into two divisions, National League East and National League West. Sportswriters made tired jokes about the expansion helping the Mets—they would never finish lower than sixth again. Tom spared himself from these writers by keeping his predictions private.

Instead, he simply announced, "I want to be the best ballplayer, the best pitcher, Tom Seaver can possibly be." The other players, including Grote, Harrelson, Jones, and Agee, shared this attitude. They believed if each Met fulfilled his promise, they could top the division that now included the New York Mets, the Chicago Cubs, the St. Louis Cardinals, the Montreal Expos, the Pittsburgh Pirates, and the Philadelphia Phillies.

Despite their faith in themselves, no one shared their optimism. Most people still expected them to lose. Even Gil Hodges, who had recovered completely from his heart attack, had set a modest goal of eighty-five victories for the Mets. The team, however, set out to win a championship, not a .500 season.

On opening day, it was the Mets versus the Montreal Expos at Shea. Thirty-five thousand fans came to find out if the Mets could break their opening-day jinx and beat the rookie team.

The game ranked with the Met absurdities of earlier years. Tom, pitching the opening game again, was less than terrific. The Expos shelled him and others for eleven runs, while the usually low-scoring Mets squandered ten runs to lose 11–10. "My God, wasn't that ridiculous?" Tom said after the game.

When reporters asked Hodges what he thought, he said, "What can I say? I think anytime the Mets give Tom ten runs again he'll win the game."

But victories continued to elude the Mets all of April. Despite the powerful pitching of Tom, Jerry Koosman, Nolan Ryan, and Tug McGraw, they struggled to break even. They still missed double plays, overthrew in the clutch, and missed coaching cues. "They look like the old Mets," the writers sneered.

Gil Hodges, usually patient, had seen enough one night. The Mets had thrown away a game to the Braves with errors and dumb plays. They had lost in their usual one-run way 6–5. After the game he excused the attendant and closed the clubhouse door. He spoke quietly, but no one in the room misunderstood his rage. Tom listened, head bowed. An awkward silence followed Gil's speech until Tom cleared his throat and declared, "We needed that. I expect it to help us."

He was right, because although the Mets didn't go on a blazing winning streak, they did start to win more than they lost. In May, Tom shut out Atlanta 3–0 and brought the Mets to 18 wins against 18 losses.

After the game, the sportswriters crowded into the locker room. Jack Lang of *The Sporting News* shouted, "Tom! You're a .500 ball club! Aren't you going to celebrate?"

"What's so good about .500?" he demanded. "That's only mediocre. We didn't come into this season to play .500 ball." The clubhouse had become deathly quiet. The reporters looked surprised, but Tom's teammates agreed with every word. "I'm tired of the jokes about the old Mets," he went on. "Let Rod Kanehl and Marvelous Marv laugh about the Mets. We're out here to win. You know when we'll have champagne?" he paused. "When we win the pennant."

"Great," said Maury Allen, shrugging his shoulders. "But I'll be too old to enjoy it." For a while, Maury Allen seemed prophetic as the Mets lost their next five games. Success had gone to their heads, the press suggested.

The Giants and Dodgers came to New York at the end of May, each to play a three-game series with the Mets. Because both had been New York teams before moving away, their games always attracted sell-out crowds that usually watched the slaughter of the Mets. This year the Mets were determined to even the score, if only by a little, with their big brothers.

Tom, Harrelson, and Nancy with Met founder Joan Whitney Payson

On May 30th, Tom pitched a 4–3 opening win over the Giants, his seventh victory of the season. With the winning momentum of the first game, the Mets swept both series from the Giants and Dodgers. They had won seven in a row and were playing above .500. More important than the statistics, finally they were contenders in the pennant race.

The Mets followed the Giants and Dodgers back to California and shamed the former New Yorkers again. In San Francisco, they won their eleventh straight game, setting a Met record, and jumped into second place behind the front-running Chicago Cubs. By the time they traveled back to Shea to meet the Cubs, they were just five games out of first place.

The Cubs began the season with a tremendous head start over the other clubs and were determined to crush the upstart Mets. Their controversial manager, Leo Durocher, added fuel to the fire. Because he had managed both the Brooklyn Dodgers and the New York Giants, at least half of New York always hated him. Now, all New York cast Leo as the villain.

The Mets, or the New Breed, as Casey Stengel called them, didn't care too much about the old feud between Durocher and New York, but they did want the division championship and felt they could snatch it from the Cubs. Tom, pitching strongly, was winning consistently. Jerry Koosman and Gary Gentry were pitching beautifully, and Nolan Ryan's fastball was smoking past the batters. Besides pitching, the Mets, especially Tommy Agee, were hitting. The outfield was slugging home runs, and the infield had tightened its defense. Nevertheless, Durocher and his Cubs came to Shea expecting to fatten their lead.

On July 9th, a record number 59,083 Metsomaniacs, as they proudly called themselves, came to watch Tom duel with the Cubs. Tense and moody all that day, Tom warmed up for a long time, worrying about some stiffness in his shoulder. The last thing he needed on a night like this was arm trouble.

In the bottom of the first inning, he watched with relief as Tommy Agee tripled on Ken Holtzman's first pitch. Third baseman Bobby Pfeil hit the next ball for a double and Agee scored. The crowd roared. "At least some of the heat is off me," Tom told himself, as he trotted out to the mound to face the Cubs.

His arm loosened and he retired the Cubs one, two, three. Happily, he looked up behind home plate and found Nancy sitting with his father, who was visiting from California. She tipped her tam-o'-shanter cap to him, and he touched the brim of his cap to say, "I'm fine." The Mets scored two more runs in the second inning.

By the sixth inning, Tom hadn't given up a hit or a walk. Each time he threw the ball, the fans became quietly attentive—he was close to a perfect game. A perfect game happens once every 10,000 games. The National League didn't even have a perfect game until 1964, when Jim Bunning of the Phillies pitched one against the tenth-place Mets.

When Tom came out to the mound a little after ten

o'clock, he was just three outs away from the perfect game. He paused, massaging a new ball for a moment, to look things over. Fans were standing behind the last row of seats all the way down the left-field and right-field lines screaming their heads off. He had never seen such wild enthusiasm, and it excited him. His heart pounded and his arm felt weightless, as though it could float from his shoulder any minute.

He looked up into the stands, at the people on their feet, roaring and tearing the place apart, and he thought, "Moments like these are reserved for other people—they're for the Sandy Koufaxes and Mickey Mantles and Willie Mayses of this world. Not for the Tom Seavers and the New York Mets." Yet, Tom wanted that game more than anything he'd ever wanted in baseball, and he was determined to have it.

The first man up, Randy Hundley, bunted right to Tom. He took his time and threw the ball to Donn Clendenon at first base for an easy out.

"I can have it, I can have it, I can have it," he chanted to himself after the play.

Jimmy Qualls, a rookie batting .243, was up next. Tom had never seen him bat until then. His first time up he had lined out with a long flyball to Ron Swoboda in right field.

With two outs to go, Tom threw his first pitch carefully, a sinker, but the ball didn't sink. It came in waist high over the plate. Catcher Jerry Grote wanted to dash out and grab the ball before it reached Qualls, but Qualls swung hard and slammed the ball into left

		21 RF					
3 3		9 C					
0 1		42 CF	AT BAT II	BALL 0	STRIKE 2		OUT 2
1 11		25					
0 9			1 2 3 4 5 6 7 8 9 10			R	H
3 10		HE	CHI . CUBS	· 0 0 0 0 0 0 0 ·		0	1
0 12			N . Y . METS	1 2 0 0 0 0 1 0 ·		4 8
2 12			CUBS HERE TOMORROW AFTERNOON				

The end of the "almost perfect" game

field. It dropped between Jones and Agee and the perfect game was finished.

Tom couldn't believe it. As he watched Jones field the ball, he felt empty and numb with all his adrenaline gone. Almost mechanically, he got the next two batters out.

He walked to the clubhouse, head down, disappointment choking him. He smiled weakly as the other players clapped him on the back. Nancy was standing by the clubhouse door, crying. "What are you crying for?" he said to her, near tears himself. "We won, four to nothing."

The one-hitter moved the Mets within three games of the Cubs, and the sting of the near-perfect game eased as they drew closer to first place. The Cubs won the next day, but the Mets then beat the Expos two out of three. Chicago was their next stop, and the papers speculated whether the young Mets would fold under the pressure. They lost their first game in Chicago with Tom pitching 1–0. A writer asked Durocher, "Were those the real Cubs today?"

"No," he snapped. "Those were the real Mets today."

The Cub manager was no judge of reality. The intrepid Mets hovered near the Cubs in their race for first place. On September 10th, the Mets faced a crucial double-header against the Astros at Shea. If they could sweep the Astros, they would nudge the Cubs from first place. In fact, if the Phillies could beat the Cubs that afternoon, the Mets would need only one win to take first place.

The Mets beat the Astros in the first game 3–2, but no one relaxed. Everyone watched the scoreboard with the Cub-Phillies scores just as closely. They were tied 2–2 until in the middle of the Mets' second game, the scoreboard flashed, "Phillies 6, Cubs 2." The stadium erupted as fans cheered, wept, and waved banners proclaiming, "We're Number 1!"

Moments later the Mets had won their second game. While the fans ran down to the field to grab souvenirs, the players celebrated in the clubhouse with a single bottle of champagne and many high hopes.

Tom had already surpassed his goal of 20 games— he had won 25—but like all the Mets he was trying to

After winning his 20th

figure out the magic number, the number of games they needed to clinch the division. On September 25th, the moment arrived when the Mets beat the Cardinals 5–0 at Shea Stadium. Tom yelled, "Champagne, baby!" and dashed to the clubhouse. Champagne annointed the players, sprayed the television cameras, and drenched everyone in sight. The writers who crowded among the players were exultant, too. They had watched the hapless Mets go from being the very worst team in baseball to first in their division. Marvelous Marv was fun, but those old days didn't compare to the glory of this team of Seaver, Koosman, Agee, and the rest.

Carefully, Bud Harrelson worked his way through the crowd with a brimming glass of champagne for Mayor Lindsay. Just as he was about to offer it to him, Tom dispensed with formalities and poured a chilling bottle of champagne over the Mayor of New York's head. While the Mayor sputtered, Tom was busy dousing Gil Hodges's head as the manager talked into a TV microphone. "Congratulations, Gil," Tom yelled, just before Jerry Grote doused the 25-game winner with his own shower of champagne.

8 . . .
Met Magic

The playoffs against the Western Division champions, the Atlanta Braves, quickly sobered Tom. He always respected Henry Aaron, Orlando Cepeda, and Rico Carty, and the playoffs intensified the challenge.

On October 4th, Tom awoke early in Atlanta, his mind and body in knots. He would open the five-game playoff series at four in the afternoon. He mumbled "Good morning" to Nancy and left before she could answer. The late playoff time increased his nervousness; he hated waiting all afternoon. Usually, he welcomed the butterflies as a sign he was ready for a game, but today they overwhelmed him. His mouth was dry, his hands clammy, his eyes glazed. The warm, sticky weather bothered Tom, too. He'd grown used to pitching in cool fall weather, and found that heat tired him out faster.

On the team bus, he listened with half an ear to the chatter around him. Bud Harrelson, sitting next to him, was used to Tom's silence before a game, but

Tom seemed especially removed today. He was thinking about Henry Aaron. "I can't let him hurt us, I can't give him anything good," he told himself.

The tension still clung to him during the warmup practice. He hoped it would fade after the first pitch. Felix Millan faced Tom first. Tom struck him out, but, surprisingly, remained nervous. The tension had tightened his body and was interfering with his pitching. He was rushing his motion and delivering too quickly with the ball low. Catcher Jerry Grote came out to him and advised Tom to get his arm up higher. But when he did get the ball higher, it hung there for base hits. By the seventh inning the score was tied 4–4.

Henry Aaron strode to the plate. He had singled once already. Tom felt his heart pounding. "I won't let him hit me," he told himself, as he began to pitch around Aaron. Aaron, canny as ever, expected the slow outside curve, and slammed the ball out of the park for a home run. Tom got through the rest of the inning safely, but the damage was done—the Braves had the lead 5–4.

When the Mets were up in the eighth, Gil took Tom out and brought in J. C. Martin to pinch-hit. Martin began a rally that ended with five runs, and the Mets snatched the victory from the Braves 9–5. The Braves were beginning to believe in Met Magic.

After the game the reporters crowded around Tom. "Do you think your problem out there was because you hadn't played in a week?" one reporter suggested. It was a tempting alibi, an easy way of blaming his trouble on the manager.

"No. I tried to control my nerves and I couldn't," he admitted. "I was more tense than usual and more nervous."

The Mets swept the series, three in a row, beginning with Tom's game, then Koosman's 11–6 victory, and finishing with Gary Gentry's 7–4 win.

By the time the Mets were to face the American League pennant winners, the Baltimore Orioles, for the World Series Tom's nerves had toughened. If the Mets could beat Atlanta without their best effort, he reasoned, they could certainly beat the Orioles. Beyond that, when he arrived at Memorial Stadium in Baltimore, the thrill of just being in the World Series erased his worries. He couldn't wait to face them.

The Baltimore press described the contest as ridiculous, as almost embarrassing that the ace Orioles would have to play the clownish Mets. "Met Miracle Story Nearing End," the headline proclaimed. Tom decided to get even with the paper.

After breakfast the Mets piled into a bus to go to the ballpark for a long warm-up practice the day before the first game. In the clubhouse, Tom and Gary Gentry switched jerseys, Tom wearing Gary's number 39 and Gary wearing Tom's number 41. The Baltimore reporters, spotting 41, thought it was Tom Seaver and came over to ask him questions about Gary Gentry. Number 41 declared, "I think Gary Gentry is a lousy pitcher."

The surprised writers, who didn't know much about Tom Seaver (not even what he looked like), had heard Tom was a sweet kid from California. They certainly didn't expect him to attack another player. They were all scribbling furiously when a *New York Times* writer passed by and said to number 39, "Hi, Tom." The Baltimore writers stopped writing long enough to glare at the real Tom Seaver, who was displaying a puckish grin.

The next morning, however, Tom was in no playful mood. Ready to pitch the first game against the Orioles, he felt his normal nervousness. His edginess increased as he sat in the hotel coffee shop waiting to be served breakfast. It was already 9:45 and the bus would be leaving soon. He saw Bud down there also waiting for breakfast. "Forget it," Bud said. "I've been here for fifteen minutes and they haven't looked at me yet."

When he got to the stadium, Tom gulped down a roast beef sandwich and began to analyze the game. Don Buford, curve balls. Paul Blair, fastball hitter, curves to him, too. Frank Robinson, powerful—breaking balls outside the plate for him. Boog Powell, a monster, crowds the plate, jam him. No mistakes with him or he'll hit the ball 800 miles.

Tom respected the lineup, but it didn't overwhelm him. Thinking about each hitter calmed him, because it took his mind off the importance of the game. By measuring their strengths against his, he brought the game down to a level he could understand, the battle of the pitcher against his natural enemy, the hitter.

The first Oriole batter was Don Buford. Buford had gone to U.S.C. a few years before Tom, and Rod Dedeaux had flown to Baltimore to watch two of his Trojans do battle. Tom had watched Buford on television, and from the way he moved into a pitch, he was sure his fastball would work. The first pitch was inside for a ball, but Tom felt the nervousness leave him with the pitch. The next pitch was a fastball. Buford expected the pitch, and connected solidly. The ball sailed high into right field. Tom waited for Ron Swoboda to get under it, but it was taking too long. "What in the world is going on," he wondered. And then he saw Ron vainly leap as the ball cleared the fence.

Incredible. A home run on the second pitch. "Another Met record," Tom thought wryly. He had relaxed for a moment, but the home run started everything moving in him. Boom! His heart pounded; anger burned his ears. He got out of the inning quickly, but one run behind.

The Mets lost the game 4–1, but for Tom it was the first time in his life that defeat didn't depress him. Even though it was his first loss after eleven victories, just to have pitched in the World Series was enough. "I'm the first man in the history of the New York Mets to lose a World Series game," he joked afterwards.

Part of Tom's cheerfulness also came from seeing that Baltimore wasn't such a powerhouse after all. The Mets almost beat them, and with a couple of breaks they could have won. Tom was sure the Mets would win the Series.

That night Tom went to dinner in Baltimore with his entire family—Nancy, his parents, his brother and sisters and their spouses. Mr. Seaver remarked, "I guess it takes a World Series to get us all together again." Tom smiled and looked around the room.

He spotted Rod Dedeaux and Justin sitting with that other Trojan, Don Buford. "Front-runner," Tom kidded Don and slapped him on the back.

Their former coach nodded approvingly. Rod had seen enough athletes to know the importance a sense of humor plays in bearing the frustration and depression of losing. "You need to have the world broad enough around you so you don't feel it will come to an end when you lose," Rod would tell his team.

Jerry Koosman taught the Orioles about Met Magic the next day when he polished them off 2–1 with a two-hitter. The next three games were at Shea, and the Mets hoped they could finish the Series on home ground with their adoring fans.

The Mets easily won the third game 5–0 with a 400-foot home run by Tommy Agee. By now everyone in New York, from dress designers to cab drivers, was following the saga of the Mets. New Yorkers were taking the rise of the Mets personally and hoped Tom Terrific would show Baltimore the "real Tom Seaver," in the fourth game.

When he awoke October 15th he felt relaxed and

rested after sleeping ten hours. He got up, put his head out the window and was relieved to feel cool weather. He left for Shea early to talk to Gary Gentry about how he had struck out Don Buford the day before.

When he arrived at 10:00 A.M., a huge crowd of people was already waiting outside the park. As he walked toward the entrance, he heard, "Just one, See-vuh!" over and over as fans shoved baseballs and paper at him to sign. He loved being a hero, but today he wanted to be left alone, to prepare mentally and emotionally for this all-important game. If he won, the Mets would be only one game away from being World Champions. He hurried past the crowd, smiling but not stopping for a second.

He warmed up in the bullpen, his arm loose, his timing right, but his stomach fluttery. At exactly one o'clock, Tom sprinted from the bullpen to the mound to show the Orioles he was ready. The first batter was Buford. Tom wound up and threw a fastball that Buford took for a strike, and Tom relaxed. He began to think that in thirty hours, after he had beaten the Orioles and Koosman had beaten them the next day, the Mets would be the baseball champions of the world. But in the ninth inning the score was tied 1–1.

In the bottom of the ninth, he sat in the dugout praying for the Mets to score and end the game. Although two men got on base, they couldn't get one home, so the game went into extra innings. Without looking at Gil, Tom put on his glove and walked reso-

Pitching the final game of the World Series

lutely to the mound. He wanted to finish the game, and if he looked questioningly at Hodges, he might be taken out.

The Orioles had their best hitters for this tenth inning. Dave Johnson hit a grounder for a single. Tom knew Mark Belanger, the next batter, would try a bunt. He pitched a high fastball that Belanger could only nick, and Jerry Grote caught the pop-up for an out. Then pinch-hitter Clay Dalrymple singled to left and Johnson moved to second. Rube Walker came out and asked Tom how he felt. "I'm tired, but I've got a few pitches left," he said.

Buford was up next. On an outside pitch Buford hit the ball hard into right field. Tom held his breath. Swoboda caught the ball, but Johnson tagged up and reached third. One more out, Tom told himself. He was breathing heavily, and his fastballs were slowing down. He'd have to try a breaking pitch on Paul Blair. It worked, and he struck him out.

Tom walked quickly into the dugout, listening to the applause. Jerry Grote was up. "C'mon, Jerry," he shouted desperately, "Hit a double!" Grote popped an easy fly ball into left field. Tom's heart sank, but Met Magic struck. Buford, the left fielder, lost the ball in the sun and dropped it. By the time the ball was fielded, Grote was on second. Gil sent in Rod Gaspar to pinch-run for Grote.

The Oriole pitcher, Pete Richert, deliberately walked Al Weis to set up a double play. J. C. Martin, pinch-hitting for Tom, bunted a fastball right near home plate. The pitcher scooped up the ball and threw to first, but the ball ticked Martin's wrist and fell. Tom remembered, "I knew right then, as soon as I spotted the loose ball, that we had won the game. I turned my eyes and picked up Gaspar, halfway down the line between third and home. All I could see was home plate and his legs, and then as his front foot stretched out and touched the plate, my whole baseball life flashed in front of me. The perfect game I pitched when I was twelve, my grand-slam home run in Alaska, my first Met game, my almost-perfect game against the Cubs—all those minor miracles led to the one magic day."

After a grand celebration dinner with his family, he and Nancy went home, physically exhausted but emo-

Champagne celebration

tionally soaring. On their door, they found a huge sign painted by a neighbor. It read, "Nice going, Tom, we knew you could do it." Tom carried the sign inside to save with his other souvenirs; however, he wouldn't need any tangible reminders of the season. Like a first love, the Mets' rise was something that happens only once, and Tom would always treasure the memory.

The next day the Mets climaxed their impossible dream with a 5–3 victory over the Orioles.

1969, the year of the Mets' triumph, was also a year of personal triumph for Tom. His 25–7 record, with a 2.21 E.R.A. and 208 strikeouts, made him the Hickok Pro Athlete of the Year, *The Sporting News* Man of the Year, and the *Sports Illustrated* Athlete of the Year. The crowning glory of his brilliant season, however, was the Cy Young Award given to him by sportswriters for being the most outstanding pitcher of the year. All year they had written about Met Magic, and now they had acknowledged the magician.

9 . . .
"Just One, See·vuh"

The wind blew briskly as Tom and Nancy hurried into Lum's, their favorite Chinese restaurant. Tom quickly scanned the place to see if his sister and brother-in-law had arrived. He was looking forward to a quiet, private evening with them.

Ever since the Mets had won the World Series three months before, Tom and Nancy had become busy celebrities giving interviews, posing for magazine covers, and taping television shows. Fame was thrilling, but sometimes they missed their privacy. They had bought a lovely old house in Greenwich, Connecticut, which they yearned to paint and fix up, but they barely had time even to sleep in it.

Being a celebrity also strained close relationships. Tom had seen his brother, Charles, stare at him as though he were a stranger when he was mobbed by fans screaming for autographs.

Owner George Lum spotted Tom and Nancy at the door and seated them in a large booth. Suddenly, a huge fat woman and her husband jumped into the empty seats in the booth. Without introduction, the lady started to tell Tom her family's history and how much they loved baseball. After listening for a minute or two, Tom looked away to keep from laughing. By now Carol and Bob had arrived, and were waiting to sit down. Nancy looked at them, helplessly.

"Oh, these must be your seats," the lady said, turning around. "Sorry," she said, and left as abruptly as she had arrived.

Such incidents flattered and amused Tom, but some of the thrill of being a hero had already worn off. Most people didn't know anything about him as a person and really didn't care. "Do they think I'm only a ballplayer?" he wondered. His answer came when he went to a newsstand to buy a paper and saw his face on the cover of four baseball magazines. He bought them all, curious to read what these writers, who had never met him, would say.

The Mets began the 1970 season like the World Champions they were, with Tom winning his first two games. Despite the busy winter that kept him from exercising, he felt strong and confident he would have another exceptional year.

The year-old San Diego Padres faced Tom at Shea for his third start. He was as controlled as ever, but in the fourth inning, catcher Jerry Grote became aware of the speed he was putting on the ball—it blurred as it crossed the plate.

Clowning with Rube Walker while wearing the coach's old uniform

By the seventh inning he had struck out thirteen batters. The year before, Phillies pitcher Steve Carlton set the record by striking out nineteen Mets. Tom knew he was throwing hard, but he didn't know he was close to the record until Gil Hodges told him about it in the dugout.

The ball kept smoking across the plate, nicking the corners. The fans were entranced, watching Tom hurl a 5.2 ounce ball 60 feet, 6 inches, within a quarter-inch of any area of the plate. Over and over he stymied the batters with his razor-sharp fastball that came nowhere near the fat of the bat. A radar machine timing his pitches clocked some at 105 miles per hour.

With two out in the ninth inning, he had struck out a total of 18 men. He needed one more strikeout to tie the record. Al Ferrara was up. Tom knew better than to throw him a fastball. He had hit one for a home run in the second inning. He sent him a slider, a fastball that veered at the last moment. Strike one. "Good," Tom thought to himself. "I'll send him another slider." But this one was too far outside, and Ferrara let it go for a ball. Without wasting a moment, Tom slipped him a fastball for strike two. Tom thought for a moment as he stepped off the mound. He zipped him another fastball. Only its seams crossed the plate. The batter went down swinging, and the crowd, which had been tense and silent watching the performance, erupted with a standing ovation. They had watched Tom strike out ten men in a row and tie the record for strikeouts in a nine-inning game. Undefeated in his

Approaching his 19th strikeout as he pitches in the ninth inning, April 22, 1970

last ten games of 1969 and his first three games of 1970, he had just won his thirteenth game in a row. "When are you going to lose, Tom?" a reporter asked him.

"It'll happen," Tom said, grinning after his performance, but it didn't happen until three games later, when he lost 3–0 to Montreal.

The better he pitched, the more he expected of himself. He wanted to win thirty games that year. "A normal game for me," he told one reporter, "is five hits and ten strikeouts." The reporter was surprised. Tom had always been confident and professional, but now he was beginning to sound cocky. If he walked three batters he complained it was too many. After a one-hit, 15-strikeout game against Philadelphia, he was angry with himself. "I wasn't perfect," he complained after the game.

Tom's stress on perfection began to affect his moods. He became more emotional publicly, especially after losing, and the press called him on it. Jack Lang of *The Sporting News* wrote: "Losing appears to be getting to Seaver. He is not reacting to adversity as well as he did to success. He appeared in his first three years to be impervious to faults, but in his fourth season he is showing another side of Tom, a not-so-pleasant side."

The constant eye of the newspapers intensified his edginess. After losing a close game, he'd go back to the clubhouse, wanting to be alone. But before he could sit down, a circle of reporters would ask him a dozen questions about why he hadn't been perfect. If he spoke too quickly, he'd find his words in a headline the next day.

Losing games was often frustrating, because the Mets weren't scoring runs. If he gave up five hits, he could easily lose a game. His record slipped to 7–5. In the five losing games the Mets scored a total of two runs. The weak-hitting club, the nosy press, and most of all his demand for perfection, obscured the joy of baseball for Tom.

1970 Met All Stars (from left to right) Bud Harrelson, Tug McGraw, Gil Hodges, Joe Pignatano, trainer Tom Mc-Kenna, Seaver, and Ron Taylor

Then the Mets began hitting again and were within two-and-a-half games of first place by mid-August. Tom's record stood at 17 wins, 6 losses. If he kept winning, he'd reach 30. Gil Hodges and Rube Walker asked Tom if he'd like to pitch three times in ten days instead of twice. They wanted to close the gap between them and the first-place Pirates and felt Tom could do it.

Tom liked the idea because it gave him an extra chance to reach 30, but he was to learn that he needed the five-day rotation. The first night Tom was ahead 2–1 in the ninth inning in Atlanta, when he missed Jerry Grote's two fingered cue for a curveball. He whipped in a fastball that took Grote by such surprise he lost the ball, and two runs scored before he found it. The Mets lost 3–2.

Three days later Tom pitched against the Astros and gave up nine runs for a 9–4 loss. The third game he pitched and lost 7–5, again to the Astros. The three games shook his confidence and exhausted him. He couldn't find his rhythm and strength after those games and won only one more that season. His slump, which gnawed at him constantly, hurt the team as it struggled to overtake the Pirates. The Mets ended up in second place and Tom finished with a disappointing 18–12 record.

Gil Hodges had his opinion of Tom's trouble. He didn't think it was Tom's delivery or anything that was physically wrong. Instead, he explained, "He's a perfectionist who over-concentrated and lost some of his natural command, like a hitter in a slump. He was always trying to be perfect, to be analytical, to be Tom Seaver."

Tom overheard this and shrugged his shoulders. All he knew was that he was tired, more tired than he'd ever been before. First his body had given him signals, and then mentally he just couldn't concentrate. What he and Nancy needed was to get away from New York for awhile, from the pressure of being Tom Seaver. The World Series, the busy winter that followed, and the 1970 season, had overwhelmed him. "I have to rest and start again," he told friends.

So he and Nancy took a rambling trip across the United States with Fresno as their ultimate destination to restore themselves and remember what life was about. The first stop in remote Ashfield, Massachusetts, brought them to Charles, who had left the city's distractions to concentrate on his art. Eight years younger than Charles, Tom had learned many things from his older brother. Here, away from New York, Tom watched him sculpt for hours, without pressure, and learned another lesson. He had pushed himself too hard the past year. It was time to stop and look at his life. "Instead of flowing downriver with the current, I'll sit back and evaluate things," he told Charles. Tom admired Charles' life-style, but it wasn't for him. Tired as he was, he already missed playing baseball.

The next stop took them to Cooperstown, New York, home of the Baseball Hall of Fame. Tom walked into the room filled with mementoes of baseball legends like Babe Ruth, Lou Gehrig, Ty Cobb, and felt as if he had walked into one of his childhood dreams. Stan Musial's bat, Babe Ruth's gloves, Ted Williams' spikes. Incredible. He walked a little further and saw a familiar object. His cap, the one he wore when he pitched nineteen strikeouts, sat in a glass case. With all his dreams, none were big enough to imagine his cap there, side-by-side with the giants of baseball.

Suddenly, he wanted certain people to see that cap—his parents, his brother and sisters, Rod Dedeaux, and of course, Nancy. It was his hat, but without them, it wouldn't have been in Cooperstown.

By the time Tom and Nancy returned to Greenwich a month later, Tom knew who he was again. He had

Enjoying his first major league home run, July 9, 1970

been greedy in 1970 and, with the help of the press, thought he could beat every team every time. The papers and fans called him invincible, and he tried to prove it; however, the trip had reminded him of his limitations. The papers could write what they wanted —Tom had learned to separate himself from the public Tom Seaver in the press whom he did not recognize.

10 . . .
Magic 20

The phone rang at 2:00 A.M. Tom, in the St. Petersburg Hilton, answered it gruffly. It was Nancy. "Tom, I think I'm having the baby," she said.

"No, no, it's nothing," Tom replied, sleepily. He wanted to finish his dream. "Call me at four."

Promptly at 4:00 A.M. she called him again and said she was still in labor. "Honey," he said, "I can't do anything, anyway. Call me at seven."

Nancy fumed. Could this be the man who went to natural childbirth classes with her? He actually sounded annoyed she had called him. At six she called and coldly informed him she was leaving for the hospital. This time Tom finally got the message. "Okay," he assured her. "I'll grab the next plane."

He dashed to the airport, got a plane, and landed in Newark in the midst of a blizzard. He drove right to Greenwich Hospital and changed quickly into surgical clothes so he could join Nancy in the labor room. He walked in, looking tan and fit from Florida.

Nancy, white and sweating, took one look at him and said, "Oh, no, you make me sick."

He laughed and immediately set to work as her coach. He took his handkerchief and patted away the beads of perspiration on her forehead. She looked like she'd just run fifty windsprints, he noticed with surprise. Suddenly she turned to face him and said, exasperated, "I quit!"

"Nancy, there are a lot of things you can do," he told her patiently, "but right now you can't quit. You have to have this baby." Shortly after the coach's pep talk Nancy settled down and delivered a healthy, howling Sarah Lynn Seaver.

Tom stayed with Nancy and their daughter for five days, and each day he ran at the local elementary school. He had completed his job successfully as childbirth assistant, but in February, 1971, his other job would just be beginning.

"Hey, chubby right-hander, let's see if you can fool the attendance today and hit a ball past the mound," Bud Harrelson yelled from behind the batting cage. Tom grinned at him, then turned back to face the batting practice pitcher. He turned his cap back to front, swung, and weakly popped a ball behind second base that should have been caught. He protested loudly being called out, because he lost his turn in the cage.

Playful and relaxed during practice, Tom wasn't pitching that day. But even when he was pitching during the season, he wasn't pressing as hard as in 1970. Instead of demanding perfection in each pitch, he worked on what he called, "a level of concentration I can reach in each game." More than anything, he wanted the consistency of performance he admired in an athlete like the golfer, Jack Nicklaus. If Tom could pitch well for ten years, he'd be happy. Someone else could strive for the perfect game.

He wasn't worried about numbers anymore either. If he was consistent, in the end the numbers would be there. Still, he knew twenty victories, a goal set 100

(*left to right*) *Jon Matlack, Jerry Koosman, Seaver, and Tug McGraw*

years before, marked the great pitcher. Consistent performance satisfied Tom, but to prove he was a pitcher for the ages, he would have to win twenty games in 1971. He was sure he could do it.

The year started badly, however. Tom was pitching better than ever, but he wasn't winning. By early August, his record stood at 11–8. In most of the losses, he had given up three or fewer runs. "But it doesn't matter how good you pitch if you don't win," he snapped angrily at a reporter who had praised him for a well-pitched game the Mets lost.

By mid-September his record rose to 18–8. By now he could make the twenty victories, but his margin for error allowed for only one loss in three games. He lost the first start, but beat the Pirates five days later 3–1 for his nineteenth victory.

He won his twentieth victory at Shea against the Cardinals 6–1. He walked off the mound glad he had won the twenty, but he didn't need the number to know he had pitched his best year. He had struck out 289, had walked only 61, and finished the season with the lowest E.R.A. in both leagues, 1.76.

It was early April, a beautiful time of the year to be in Greenwich, but Tom was restless. He wanted to be where he belonged, in Florida, getting ready for opening day, 1972, but the Player's Association had called a strike. Distractedly, Tom worked around the house, painting, and playing with Sarah.

He was at his desk when Bud Harrelson called. "Hi, Roomie, how are you?" Tom said.

Bud asked tensely, "Have you heard the news?" Tom, thinking the baseball strike was over and the season would begin on time, said, "It's all settled?"

"No," Bud said. "Gil died."

"What?" Tom said, not believing what he had heard. "What do you mean, died? I just saw him two days ago. He looked great."

"He had a heart attack playing golf in West Palm Beach," Bud replied. Tom's picture of Gil, tanned and healthy, didn't fit Bud's words. He hung up the phone and sat for a long time, thinking how baseball would be without the man who had taught him so much.

The strike ended but the season opened sadly, with all the Mets mourning Gil Hodges. It was up to Yogi Berra, the new manager, to pull the club together. He struggled from the beginning of the delayed season to overcome the loss of Gil and to cope with an epidemic of hurt players. The sportswriters predicted a dismal year, but the Mets fooled them. Their morale was high, and although they weren't scoring runs, they were playing a tight defensive game that put them in a pennant race with the Pirates again.

Tom, however, was struggling, and wasn't helping the team as much as he wanted to. His timing was off too many times, and he could only finish two of his first ten starts. But once in awhile everything was right, and he was grateful. He was thrilled when he struck out seven and gave up only five hits, a great change over the early days of expecting each performance to be that good. Consistency eluded him, but fortunately this year the Mets weren't depending upon Tom's arm to win.

One of the reasons the Mets were winning despite Tom's struggles was Willie Mays. That spring the San Francisco Giants finally agreed to return Willie to New York, where he was still loved. He had left with the Giants after the 1957 season, but the fans had never forgotten him. The owner of the Mets, Joan Whitney Payson, was an old Giant fan who wanted Willie back for more than sentimental reasons. Despite being 41, Willie still swung a mighty bat.

The younger players, like Tom, loved having him in the clubhouse. After Mays had gotten on base 14 times out of 27 at bats, someone in the clubhouse suggested him as Player of the Month.

Tom interrupted, "You can't be Player of the Month, Willie. No man over 40 is eligible."

Willie charged Tom, shouting, "Who say so . . . you say so, Seaver—that's all you know . . . rookie."

Tom rocked with laughter that began from the bottom of his toes. He'd be delighted if he could play, at 41, like Willie Mays.

A pitcher, though, often has a career shortened unexpectedly because of injuries to his arm. Tom understood at the beginning of his career the importance of being in condition, especially his legs. If his legs were weak, he tended to throw the ball too hard and get a sore arm. A sore arm could last for weeks, and the worst part was waiting and hoping for it to heal.

During spring training, Tom proceeded at the same careful pace he had the previous season, but early in training he felt a sharp pain where his shoulder and arm met. He badgered the team doctor, Dr. Peter LaMotte, with questions about what it was.

After a few days the pain held less terror, as he forced himself to understand it and learn from it. By the time it healed he could tell reporters, "I don't know many parts of my shoulder and arm, but I know this muscle, the teres major. It was bruised because I began throwing too hard too soon. I hadn't taken into consideration that I'm getting older. I can't proceed during the spring at the same pace I did at twenty-three. I have to expect my body to break down a little with each year. I just have to be more careful in the future."

By July the Mets had slipped five-and-a-half games behind the Pirates, and Tom's record was 12–7. His fastball wasn't moving consistently, and the Mets weren't hitting. "Seaver could sue the Mets for non-support and win the case without a jury," wrote the *New York Post*. Yogi Berra also felt nothing was wrong with Tom that a few runs wouldn't cure.

Tom, however, wouldn't accept Yogi's explanation. He knew the Mets; he had pitched for them for six years and had never depended on a lot of runs. He refused to speculate why this year was harder than the last, but he always welcomed his fastball when it appeared occasionally in late innings.

Once again he strove for twenty wins. Because his pitching was off, the goal tantalized him. To be consistent meant to pitch well most of the time, even when he didn't "have his stuff." Game by game he struggled and ended up winning his 21st victory against the Pirates 5–2. His E.R.A., however, at 2.92, was the highest it had ever been since he had played for the Mets.

He had pitched better, but in many ways the year was more satisfying. He had proved to himself he could adjust to the changing fortunes of time.

11 . . .
Pennant

"It won't take more than 90 victories to win in the National League East and we can win 90 if we don't have a lot of bad injuries," Yogi told his team before their 1973 opening game at Shea against the Phillies. The Mets had come close to winning for three frustrating years. This year, with new players like Jim Fregosi, Rusty Staub, and Felix Millan, they were a stronger team. As Tom told reporters, "If we stay healthy, we can have a super team."

Tom opened the season against the Phillies' ace pitcher, Steve Carlton. Tom pitched well, but when he tired in the eighth inning, Yogi sent in Tug McGraw to protect his shutout. They won 3–0 and had played like heroes; their hopes soared toward pennant dreams.

Before May, however, the team lost Milner, Millan, and Jones for two months with injuries. The strong opening team was now weak and not hitting. Tom pitched 40 innings allowing only five earned runs, but his record stood unimpressively at 2–2. He eked out his victories with superb pitching.

When a team isn't hitting, the pressure is on the pitcher. When the Yankees were a powerhouse of sluggers, pitcher Whitey Ford could leave a game in the seventh inning, assured of his victory. Tom, on the other hand, counted himself lucky if he had two easy games a year. With the Mets, he had to sweat every inning, every pitch.

When Bud Harrelson and Jerry Grote got hurt, Tom began to worry. It was bad enough to lose hitters, but now they were losing two superb defensive players as well. If the pitching staff weakened, the Mets would be out of the race.

Late in May, Tom beat the Pirates twice, 6–0 and 4–3. A week later he struck out 16 Giants in San Francisco and beat them 5–2. After he defeated the Padres 9–2, he had a solid 7–3 record, a 1.74 E.R.A., and led the league in strikeouts. The Mets, because of Tom, edged into third place, six-and-a-half games behind the Cubs.

Yogi was more than grateful, and confessed to reporter Jack Lang one day, "I don't know where we'd be without Tom."

Lang, who had been an early Met watcher, looked at him shrewdly and said, "In last place on a 17-game losing streak."

Late in June more of the team crumbled. The offense was still hurt, the defense was spotty, and now the relief pitching collapsed. Only Tom, Jerry Koosman, and Jon Matlack held the Mets together. As they continued to pitch masterfully, the team hovered close enough to stay in the race. By September 1st they were in last place, but only six-and-half games behind the first place Cardinals. Bud Harrelson told reporters, "Without Tom and the other pitchers, we could be out of first place by twenty-five games."

Still powerful, Tom's E.R.A. was an extraordinary 1.70, and his 15–8 record was miraculous given the team's injuries.

Now the emotional strain was beginning to show. Tom's eternal optimism was gone—he didn't think the team could pull ahead at the last minute. But suddenly the hurting Mets recovered and began to hit again. It was a good thing, because Tom, described as the team's "ten-armed lifeguard," found his arm very tired from keeping the club afloat. He couldn't wait much longer for the hot streak the Mets needed to grab first place from the Cardinals.

The turning point came in a series sweep against the Cubs, when the Mets crept to within two-and-a-half games of first place. Pennant fever infected the newly charged team. They were in fourth place September 17th, when they began a crucial series with the Pirates.

The Mets swept the Pirates, climaxed by Tom's 10–2 victory on September 21st. That victory put them in first place. The scoreboard at Shea beamed, "Look Who's Number One!," and the crowd roared its approval. Tom tipped his cap to the people who appreciated his effort as well as his success.

The race, however, was far from over. The Mets, in

first place, had a percentage of .506, while the second place Pirates had a .503 percentage with fewer losses. Chicago, the fifth-place team, was only three games out of first. On the last day of September, five teams still could clinch first place in the National League Eastern Division. All the teams were tired, but Yogi Berra was especially worried about the key strength of the Mets, the starting pitchers. They had endured an especially hard season with so little support from the team.

On Wednesday night, September 26th, Tom faced the Montreal Expos. The first pitch told him his arm was feeling the 2000 innings he had pitched in seven years. "The ball felt like a shotput," he said in the clubhouse after losing the game 8–5. He had given up three hits, five walks and five runs in two innings. It wasn't just an off night for him. He had given every bit of himself to the game, whatever was left of him this late in the season, but it wasn't enough. He was frightened, but if he had kept his composure this long, maybe he could hang on one more week.

His record, 19–10, didn't tell the story of his work for the team. He couldn't win twenty games this season, but his 2.08 E.R.A. and his 251 strikeouts were the best in the league. Now at the end, all he wished was that he could be part of the final push.

Monday would decide the race. The Mets had to win one of the two games they would play that day against Chicago. Despite his concern about Tom's strength, Yogi decided to start him for the opening game. The very name, Tom Seaver, was powerful enough to challenge the Cubs. Bud Harrelson, who in many ways knew Tom better than Yogi, wasn't so sure. "He got us here," Bud said, "but he's got to be tired. If he doesn't make it, I've got to sympathize with him."

On one hand, Tom loved the challenge of trying to win when he was so tired, but on the other hand, he was afraid of losing such an important game. One writer wrote, "When you get to where Tom Seaver is, it doesn't only matter how many you win, but which ones you win."

As Tom had feared, from the first inning at Wrigley Field, he was missing his fastball. He concentrated; his windup felt good, but the balls were slow and fat for hitting. The Mets were hitting, though, and in the second inning Cleon Jones hit a long home run to give the Mets a 1–0 lead. In the fourth inning Jerry Grote drove in two runs with a single and the Mets led 3–0. By the fifth inning, they were ahead 5–0. Tom was still holding the Cubs by out-foxing them with curves and sliders, but even with all those runs he didn't know if they would be enough for him that day.

In seven innings he had given up eleven hits. The Cubs picked up two runs when Rick Monday came up to bat in the bottom of the seventh. Rick, who always said "a guy would have to be crazy to want to bat against Seaver" saw Tom was tired. Maybe he'd catch a mistake. Sure enough, he found it and sent the ball into the right field seats for a home run. Tug McGraw took over and held the Cubs to win the game

6–4. The Mets bounded into the clubhouse, Tom and Tug embracing each other, while champagne poured everywhere. Somehow, they had pulled off another unexpected championship. In a few days they would challenge the powerful Cincinnati Reds for the pennant.

Tom was thrilled Yogi still wanted him to pitch the opening game against the Reds in Cincinnati. The Reds, known as the Big Red Machine, were a powerhouse of hitters. Bench, Rose, Morgan, Perez—no team was more intimidating. Tom saw all games and all teams as the same job, though. "I don't pitch harder against one team than against another team," he told a reporter. "The most important thing is not the team you're pitching against, but that it's a game to be won." Still, the drama of the playoffs and 53,000 excited fans had charged him up for this important game.

Pete Rose, the first batter, took one look at Seaver's fastball and knew he had some work to do if the Reds were going to get in front of Tom and the Mets that day. He didn't succeed, and Tom finished the first inning quickly, feeling as strong as he had in July.

Cincinnati pitcher Jack Billingham, another 19-game winner in 1973, walked Bud Harrelson in the top of the second inning. Then Tom stepped up to the plate and cracked a long base hit to center field. As he raced to second, he saw Harrelson score, giving the Mets a 1–0 lead. Grinning, Tom savored the few hits and R.B.I.'s he managed to get. It told the team he was giving his best effort all the time, not just on the

Tom facing Cincinnati in the final game of the playoffs

mound. When a pitcher hits, he believed, it rouses the team to their best effort, too.

Even though Tom had struck out twelve, by the seventh inning he was tired. When Pete Rose faced Tom again he waited for the right pitch and then sent it into the stands for a home run. The score was tied 1–1. It stayed tied until the ninth when Johnny Bench guessed right and hit Tom's inside fastball for another home run and the Reds won the game 2–1.

"How does it feel? Knocking in the only run you get? Is it frustrating?" The reporters crowded around Tom minutes after the home-run pitch. With sweat dripping into his beer, he grinned wryly. How could they ask if it was frustrating? He had pitched himself dry for four months, watched the team rise and falter a dozen times, and now he'd just lost a game in the tenth inning. "Yes," he said, straightfaced. "It's frustrating."

The frustration vanished four days later, when in the fifth and final game between the teams, Tom pitched a 7–2 victory. They had won the National League pennant and would face the Oakland A's. In the clubhouse, Tom shouted, "Fabulous!" He sipped champagne and felt the strain of the season ease. But in this celebration he felt different, almost wistful. For the first time, the clubhouse was not his ultimate reward after a well-pitched game. The reward was pitching the game and being proud of his creation. The jubilation was fun, but it was his memory of the game that he treasured.

Before the first game of the World Series, Reggie Jackson, Oakland's grand-slam slugger, quipped, "There isn't a person in the world who hasn't heard about Tom Seaver. He's so good blind people come out to hear him pitch." Maybe so, but by the end of the World Series against Oakland, Tom could only think of how nice it would be not to play baseball for awhile. The Mets lost the Series in the final inning of the seventh game. Tom pitched the third and the sixth

Tom receiving his second Cy Young Award from Joe Durso

games fairly well, but they lost both 3–2 and 3–1. He struck out 18 in the Series and gave up four earned runs in fifteen innings.

The baseball writers, appreciating Tom's extraordinary value to the Mets despite his winning only 19 games, awarded him another Cy Young Award.

Oddly enough, Tom wasn't as depressed as some of the other Mets on their sad trip back to New York. He had done his best—they all had—and they had played good ball. Like a big brother, he loved his teammates for their effort and for their appreciation of his ability. He looked forward to the next year—after he had rested.

12 . . .
Slump

His face glistening with sweat, he watched Jerry Grote's signal for a fastball. "Sure, Jerry," Tom thought bitterly, "I'd love to—I've been looking for that ball all year." With a great stride, he hurled what turned out to be a mediocre fastball. The enormous effort of pitching showed all over him. His shoulders sagged, and as he went into his usually smooth motion, he winced with each pitch. "I feel like someone is jabbing an ice pick into me, right here," Tom complained to the trainer, pointing to his left buttock.

Tom suffered this pain every time he pitched in 1974. He lost his first five games. Besides draining him physically, the pain tore at his mind, too. He was terrified by its mystery. The trainers and doctors were as baffled as Tom. He remembered that Sandy Koufax had told him that when he started to hurt he should get out of the game, but emotionally he wasn't ready to quit. Nothing satisfied Tom as much as his pitching, and he wanted to play for a long time.

The writers also mourned Seaver's problems but had little hope he would recover. They felt any pitcher who played as intensely as Tom, in which every pitch of a nine-inning game is important, has to burn out sooner or later. They had watched dozens of pitching careers come to an end through injury. Perhaps Tom Terrific's time had come, they suggested. He had nothing to regret—two Cy Youngs, three twenty-victory seasons and a lifetime 2.41 E.R.A. If he was over the hill at 30, he could exit gracefully. Their attitude disturbed Tom, but he tried not to let it affect him. The pain challenged him to remain calm. He couldn't let it interfere with his confidence, with his family, or with his team. The longer it went on, however, the harder it was to stay patient and hopeful.

The problem actually began the year before. After he had finished the exhausting 1973 season, he had a tender shoulder, which didn't surprise him. When he began spring training, he was careful not to strain it, so he eased up on throwing. Convinced his legs were most important, he neglected the conditioning of his arm. He was sure his pitches would be there when he needed them.

But the pitches eluded him. He went into his tight, fluid windup as always, but nothing happened. He had no fastball, and for a pitcher who challenged batters in a contest of power, he had to throw the ball harder.

He overstrode to get greater speed, and because of it he landed on his left heel instead of the ball of his foot. That small difference in his motion put the con-

A post-game interview

stant pounding and strain of the pitch on the wrong part of his body and threw his hips off balance. The muscles in his back pulled down and squeezed the sciatic nerve, and that was the "ice pick" Tom felt each time he pitched.

He knew he was trying to throw too hard, but it was a habit he couldn't break. Now even when he didn't overstride the pain was there. Obviously, his mechanics were wrong and he was scared, because for the first time in his pitching career he was risking an arm injury.

Tom was lucky if he won one game a month. By mid-July, the emotional strain had undermined his confidence. He had always known what he needed to do to be a good pitcher, but now he was lost. "I was just totally in the woods," he would say later.

Tom really couldn't talk to anyone about his confusion, but when his father came to New York, he found his presence reassuring. His father reminded him every athlete is entitled to an off-year. He was going through a phase, or transition, and such times are always hard. The main thing was to adjust to it, his father told him. He struggled not to take out his frustration on Nancy or Sarah, and found his family a welcome respite from pitching. They loved him with or without a fastball.

Tom endured the long season, occasionally reading the classified section of *The New York Times*, wondering what he would do if he couldn't pitch anymore. He was glad he had finally gotten his degree from U.S.C. that spring—it had taken ten years—but he still knew only baseball. In fact, he had written his geology term paper on the consistency of the National League infields.

Finally in September, Tom went to Dr. Kenneth Riland, who took one look at him and saw the trouble. "Your pelvic structure is out of balance, your hips are tilting forward," he said. "The end of my career is here," Tom thought. Tom asked him if he could help, and if he could how long it would take to cure him. The doctor, seeing Tom's fear, quickly said, "We'll straighten you out right now."

As Tom described it later, "It felt as though I got pulled around by a bulldozer." He wouldn't know if Riland had helped him until he pitched his last game of the season.

Tom hadn't been watching his statistics that year. All he knew was that with his record 10–11, the best he could do was to finish even. But when he walked into the locker room the day of his final start, the clubhouse boy, Jimmy McMahon, reminded him he still had a chance of striking out 200 if he pitched well that day. "You've got 187, Tom," the boy said, "Just 13 more." He had struck out 200 or more for six years in a row; Walter Johnson's record was seven years in a row. It was worth shooting for, as a measure of his consistency.

The moment the ball left his hand, he knew he could pitch again. The tension he carried to the game melted, and he treasured every painless pitch. He forgot about the strikeouts until he slipped into the clubhouse for a Coke during the sixth inning. The clubhouse boy rushed over with the bottle and blurted, "You're going to do it!"

In the ninth inning, Tom needed just two more strikeouts to reach 200. With his fastballs sailing in on the batters, he struck out three in a row, bringing his record to 201 and 14 for the game. The scoreboard flashed the tied record, and Tom shivered. Competing with history was awesome.

13 . . .
Triumph

Spring training tried Tom's nerves. Each time he pitched he waited, with dread, for his hip to hurt again. The long and painful '74 season had forced him to remember he couldn't pitch forever.

During the long winter that followed, Tom went home and wondered about the future. What if he couldn't make a comeback? Dr. Riland assured him he was fine, but Dr. Riland didn't have to pitch to Willie McCovey and Johnny Bench. As he watched movies for hours of himself pitching, the panic slowly disappeared. He watched each pitch he threw, and he began to see his mistakes. Now that he was well again, the mystery and fear surrounding his troubles no longer blocked his understanding.

As he watched himself over and over, he also began to appreciate the artistic part of pitching. He saw himself, with hard work, turn each pitch into a creation. Each pitch, thrown with a fresh awareness, became the sum of all previous pitches. In all the movies, he never saw the same pitch twice. There was no "usual Tom Seaver game," as though he were a machine. He discovered that he was an artist, even if his creation lasted for only an instant, and now valued his ability in a new way.

No wonder pitching excited him so much—he learned something with every pitch. He loved baseball more at 30 than at 20, and hoped he could play in '75. At the beginning of spring training, Tom told reporters, "It would be shortsighted to think all this is never going to end, but I would like a long career."

"Watch this pitch," Tom shouted to Jon Matlack, the Mets' third starting pitcher. Matlack respectfully watched as Tom went into an explosive windup in St. Petersburg. Expecting a hard thwack in his glove, Matlack braced himself, but instead the ball slipped in easily. The ball was half as fast as he expected.

"Tom," Matlack yelled, "you've got it, you've got a change-up." The one pitch Tom needed in his repertoire of fastballs, sliders, and curves, was a good change-up, a pitch thrown with the same motion as the fastball but at less speed. It fooled batters into swinging too soon. Tom's delivery had been too powerful for the change-up, but now at 30 and after last year's problems, he needed the pitch to keep on playing.

Tom had been fooling around with his grip on the ball while playing catch with Matlack. On his last pitch, he made a circle with his index finger and thumb, and put his other three fingers on the ball.

He had always used his index finger on the ball, but
he had just discovered, no matter how hard he tried,
he couldn't throw the ball hard without it. When he
showed Matlack how he did it, Matlack said, "I
wouldn't tell any kid to hold a ball that way, Tom."
Tom laughed and agreed with Jon; it wasn't a regula-
tion grip, but it worked.

Tom was not the only person rooting for his comeback. His teammates relaxed in spring training when,
by the last week of training, Tom's pitches were finally
smoking. Players like Bud Harrelson, Jerry Koosman,
and Jerry Grote wished him well not only because a
healthy Tom Seaver meant more victories, but because
they had come to love and respect him as a person.

When Tom first joined the Mets, he cared most
about his performance and winning. As he rose to star-
dom, he strove so hard for his own achievement that
he was blind to his teammates' problems. If Tom was
in a slump, he didn't notice anyone else's slump. Most
of the team accepted it as typical behavior for a star.

But as he grew comfortable with his success, he began to care about the fate of other ballplayers, especially those low on the roster. He didn't have to worry
about being cut from the team or being traded around
like a slave, but as the Met player representative, he
fought hard for the rights of the other players. Out-
spoken in his objection to the rules that took advantage
of the players, he risked the anger of the owners but
won the respect of his peers. Even the writers, who
admired Tom's talent but suspected him of shallow-

ness, saw this change and praised him for his caring and courage.

Writers and teammates joined the cheering crowd, when on July 24, 1975, Tom dramatically climbed back to strike out his 2000th victim, Cincinnati Red Dan Driessen. Soon after this milestone, the fans discovered Tom was about to break the biggest record of all, 200 or more strikeouts for eight consecutive years.

For many fans, part of baseball's appeal lies in comparing the records and performances of current players with the past. Although some die-hards wouldn't admit Tom compared to the old legends, they had to admit that after nine years his statistics crept close to setting new standards of excellence. He had proved himself worthy of the Hall of Fame and was not just a fireball pitcher for two seasons who disappears with a sore arm.

On September 1st, 52,410 people had come to Shea to see Tom pitch against the Pirates. With the Mets ahead 3–0, Manny Sanguillen, a power hitter for the Pirates, stepped to the plate. The scoreboard flashed, "This Could Be No. 200." The crowd became quiet as it concentrated on the duel. Sanguillen, determined not to make history as Seaver's strikeout victim, glared defiantly at the pitcher.

The first ball whizzed in before Sanguillen could swing. He tightened his hands on the bat and watched Seaver's motion to get a clue to the pitch. Impossible. The ball sailed in and jammed him for a second strike. Now the crowd began to rumble. With a tremendous swing, Sanguillen missed the next pitch and the rumble became a roar of appreciation for the new record and for Tom himself.

Tom stood on the mound, listening to the crowd, soaking it in and loving every moment. Jerry Grote tossed the historic ball into the dugout and came out to congratulate Tom. As Tom softly patted his friend on the back, he thought how close he had come to missing this moment.

Tom strikes out Manny Sanguillen to become the first pitcher in the history of baseball to strike out 200 or more batters a season for eight years in a row.

With his third Cy Young Award

He finished the season with a strong 22–9 record and a 2.38 E.R.A., identical to his average for his first seven years. The sportswriters honored him with a third Cy Young Award. Tom and Baltimore pitcher Jim Palmer, who received the American League Cy Young that year, were the only two men ever to have been given the award three times. Tom was thrilled by the awards, but the best part was proving he was the best pitcher in baseball.

It had been a happy year—he and Nancy had their second child, Anne Elizabeth, late in December, and Tom proved to himself he could still pitch. He only wished the Mets could have finished higher than third place, but knew it was beyond his control. He could hope, however, and he dreamed of the pennant and World Series for 1976.

14 . . .
A Classic Pitcher

It was a sunny Sunday at Shea, and if that wasn't inviting enough, the Mets were giving away bats to the children that day. In the bullpen during the pregame warm-up, Tom tried to talk to his brother, Charles, but it was impossible. Boisterous and noisy, the crowd swarmed everywhere and interrupted their conversation.

Twenty hands shoved paper at Tom, shouting at him to sign his autograph. Tom looked away, praying they would give up and leave. He loved it when someone recognized him as a person with pitching ability and asked for an autograph. But when he was in the bullpen being shouted at by fifty people, he felt like he was in a zoo, and he wasn't sure who was in the cage.

Finally, he gave up talking to Charles and got up to sign the pieces of paper thrust at him. Some of the fans, spotting Charles, shouted, "You sign, too!"

"But I'm not a player," Charles protested.

"We don't care," a man said, "sign it, anyway."

Charles took the baseball from the man reluctantly. Why would this guy want his name on a baseball? With a flourish, he signed it and handed it back to the man. It read, "The Ump."

Before they had been interrupted, Tom was telling Charles how frustrated he felt. He had won his first four games, but then the Mets had stopped hitting. Through most of July and August, he had started seven games and was charged with four losses and had three no-decisions. The frustration arose because Tom was pitching as well as he ever had. In those seven games he had given up only 13 runs. Although his E.R.A. was only 2.13, the Mets just couldn't deliver the needed runs. The year had started so brightly, but now in September he felt tired and frustrated. Except for 1969 and 1973, he dreaded September, a long, hot month if the Mets weren't in the running for a pennant.

He was still the indispensable Tom Terrific, however. For the fifth time, he won the opening game, a 3–2 victory over the Expos, and for the ninth time was selected for the All-Star team. But the thrill of baseball is winning a pennant and playing in the World Series. Breaking and setting records is exciting, but that's really a part of history. Tom missed the thrills right now. He led the National League in strikeouts; his lifetime E.R.A. was the lowest of anyone who had pitched 2000 or more innings; he had broken his own

record by striking out 200 or more batters for the ninth consecutive year, and he, like all the Mets, wanted more than anything to fight for something higher than third place. The 1976 Mets were pretty much the same Mets of 1973, and some of them who played every day like Grote and Harrelson had lost some strength. The team had become slow, and even their new manager, Joe Frazier, couldn't help them.

At times of most frustration, Tom relaxed with "his sorority house," as he called it. The change from his all-male teammates and friends delighted him. He took Sarah to ballet class and marveled that the lovely little girl was part of him.

At other times, he buried himself in books. They took his mind off the season, and they opened him to new experiences. The more aware he was of life and ideas around him, the more he valued his own art.

He wished he had learned how to play the piano. Simply to know baseball wasn't enough for him. Music, art, history—all helped him to appreciate what he was doing in his life, which included pitching.

Perhaps because the Mets gave him so little support —his record was 14–11, but his E.R.A. of 2.59 was the third lowest in the league—Tom came to value his ability separate from winning games. Always eager to pitch his own game, he could go out there, pitch the way he wanted to, and feel good about it. He never blamed his teammates for scoring only fifteen runs in the eleven games he lost.

Still, he hoped the Mets would get one or two good

Tom, Sarah Lynn, Nancy, and Anne Elizabeth at Shea

hitters for the following year. With even one more good hitter, Tom could hope for a pennant. He was 31 years old, at the peak of his career, and considered by many to be one of the finest pitchers of all time.

Tom had sweated since his Little League days to be the pitcher he knew he could be. He treasured his talent more than most, because he sacrificed so much for its development. He missed his family for five months a year; he ran windsprints in rain or blistering heat; he passed up cookies for cottage cheese; he never forgot to pet dogs with his left hand; and he endured the pressure of relentless publicity. He had played his heart out for the Mets for ten years.

Now, if the Mets continued to decline, he couldn't hope to finish higher than third place for the rest of his playing days. But he buried the thought and hoped to see new Mets the next spring.

15 . . .
Act Two

It was opening day, April 7, 1977, at Wrigley Field, Chicago. Tom walked slowly to the mound, head down, trying to forget what he had read in the paper that morning. Although he'd learned not to take the press seriously, one columnist was beginning to nettle Tom with his frequent attacks on Tom's loyalty to the Mets.

M. Donald Grant, Chairman of the Board of the Mets, had first accused Tom of disloyalty the previous year and had threatened to trade him even before they had discussed a contract. When Grant called Tom an "ingrate" Tom felt misunderstood and unappreciated, because his devotion to the team had earned him the love and respect of fans and teammates alike. Grant was unable to see that Tom was not only the pride of the Mets, but the pride of New York as well. When they finally agreed on a three-year contract, both were left feeling bitter towards one another.

Tom dreaded the long season ahead. Besides the wall between him and Grant, and constant rumors of a trade, Tom was disappointed with the 1977 team. These were his buddies, some of whom he had played with for ten years, but the Mets desperately needed new blood to tighten the defense and to spark rallies. When the free agents, those players who had played out their contracts and were free to sign with any team, were for sale during the winter, many clubs bought the stars their teams needed. But the Mets, who with a hitter or two could rise from third place to become a pennant contender, didn't get one new player.

Tom was enraged and disappointed. He had felt sure the front office would at least try to upgrade the Mets. All they needed was a little help, not an All-Star team. "We can do it," Tom told Grant. "All we need is one hitter and we're still in the race." But Grant did nothing. He seemed content with a third-place team.

Against this background, Tom pitched the opening game against the Cubs, hoping he could erase M. Donald Grant from his mind. He did. On the mound he forgot everything but the glory of pitching, and he began the season triumphantly. His tenth consecutive opener became his sixth opening day victory, 5–3.

In the home opener five days later, he shut out the St. Louis Cardinals 4–0, allowing only five hits and driving in two runs with a single. It was the Mets' third victory in four games. Euphorically, he told reporters, "Maybe I've made a mistake about our ball club." On April 17th he won his third straight game, 6–0, with a brilliant one-hitter against the Cubs for his 41st shut-out.

Congratulations from Grote after his fifth one-hitter, April 17, 1977

By May, however, the Mets began to lose steadily, and Tom's undefeated record dipped to 4–3. His frustration peaked on May 15th after he'd pitched a grueling game against the Dogers at Shea. He'd given up only one run, but in nine innings the Mets couldn't break the 1–1 tie. After twelve innings, they finally lost, 4–3, and Tom was given a "no-decision." "I worked my tail off out there today," he said. "But it was the kind of game that made me proud to be a competitor."

Abruptly, he reached into his back pocket and took out two dandelions Sarah had given him that morning, and stared at them. A reporter broke his concentration. "Can you imagine the whole year like this game?"

"Yes I can," he mumbled, still staring at the now-wilted flowers. "And it's sad." For the first time Tom Seaver felt hopeless about the Mets and his future with them.

The year before, Tom had announced on television the 1976 playoffs between the Cincinnati Reds and the Philadelphia Phillies, and he'd relished the excitement of those games. The playoffs had reminded him of what baseball was all about—the World Series. "That's the number one goal you want when you play the game. That's what makes it all worthwhile," he said later. With Grant unwilling to get a hitter to help slugger Dave Kingman and left fielder John Milner, Tom's dreams of a World Series were crushed.

The entire team suffered from the club's turmoil and morale reached a new low. By the end of May their record of 11–20 was the worst in their 16-year history.

Rumors of a Tom Seaver trade became louder in June, and Tom spoke up quickly. Because he'd played in the major leagues for at least ten years and with the same team for at least five years, he had his choice of approving which team he would be traded to. He told Grant he'd go to the Reds, Dodgers, Phillies, or Pirates —all pennant contenders. No one, including Tom, believed it would happen. "Deep down, I don't think anything is going to happen," Tom said. "Deep down, I don't want anything to happen."

Throughout the trade talks, he struggled to concentrate on his game, and on June 8th he pitched and batted the Mets to an 8–0 victory over the world-champion Cincinnati Reds. Besides holding them to

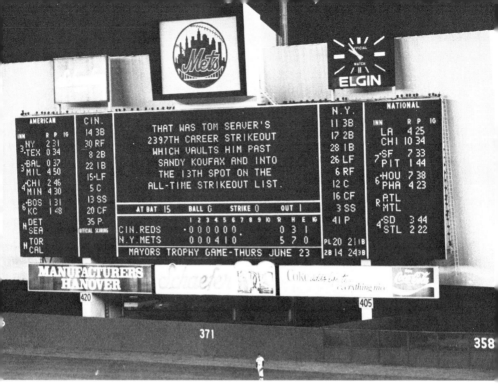

five hits and striking out ten, Tom nudged Sandy Koufax out of thirteenth place on the list of all-time strikeouts by striking out his 2,397th victim, Dan Driessen, in the seventh inning. Tom heard a roar of applause from the 23,972 fans at Shea. "It must be that cat on the field again," he said to himself, and he turned around to see. Then he glanced at the scoreboard and was thrilled to discover his new strikeout record. It was the last game Tom was to pitch for the Mets at Shea. By the end of the season he'd moved into tenth place with 2,530 strikeouts, passing Sam McDowell, Don Drysdale, and Christy Mathewson.

On Wednesday, June 15th, the agony of indecision ended when the Mets traded Tom to the Cincinnati Reds. It may have been the most unpopular trade in baseball history. New York fans, wild with anger and grief at losing their finest pitcher, jammed the Met switchboard day and night as newspapers fueled their emotions. Nearly every columnist denounced the trade as unthinkable. Ralph Nader, the consumer advocate, formed a group for fans, "to make owners think twice before they trade a popular player."

Tom's relief about leaving M. Donald Grant was tempered by his sadness at having to leave his old friends. Feeling an obligation to the press, who for the most part he felt had been fair to him, he called a press conference. When he went back to the Met clubhouse for the last time to clean out his locker, he found two dozen reporters waiting to ask questions. "Great," he thought. "The last thing I want to do is talk." But he sat down and tried to answer their queries. He answered quickly and coldly to cover his true feelings. But when one reporter asked him if he had a last word for the New York fans, Tom lost his composure. He lowered his head as his eyes flooded with tears. "The question of the fans in New York," he began, then stopped. "I know they appreciated watching me . . ." but he couldn't finish. He tapped his heart and murmured to himself, "C'mon George," but he couldn't say more.

He asked a reporter for a piece of paper and quickly scribbled, "As far as the fans go, I've given them a number of thrills, and they've been returned equally. The ovation I got the other night after passing Sandy Koufax will be one of the most memorable and warm moments of my life." He handed the paper back, walked out of the clubhouse with his duffel bag, and

UPI

Pitching his first game
as a Cincinnati Red

left the reporters to wonder about this burst of emotion from the very controlled Tom Seaver they had known for ten years.

"Johnny Bench, Ken Griffey, Pete Rose, George Foster. What a joy to have them on my side," Tom said to himself on Saturday, June 18th, in Montreal. It was his first game as a Red. He won 6–0, with a masterful three-hitter against the Expos. It was better than he expected, because the butterflies pounding his stomach in the first inning reminded him of his rookie days. But in the second inning he settled down, and before long it felt just like Tom Seaver pitching, not a Red or a Met, but himself. He also showed the Reds what a competitor he was by driving in two runs with a pair of singles. After the game he told reporters, smiling, "I'm starting the second part of my career. It's going to be beautiful."

For Tom, the season really had begun on June 15th. No longer hassled by M. Donald Grant or newspapers, Tom could settle down and play ball. Cincinnati fans welcomed him with a standing ovation before his first pitch at Riverfront Stadium, and if Tom didn't yet feel

Tom receives congratulations from Jack Billingham after his three-hit shutout against the Expos, June 18, 1977.

UPI

With Bud Harrelson before the August 21st game

at home, he certainly felt welcome. He enjoyed another welcome when he returned to Yankee Stadium two weeks later for his 11th All-Star game. For the cheering crowd, it was painful to see No. 41 doff a red cap instead of his old blue one.

Tom didn't play in New York again until August 21st, in a game against the Mets. That Sunday afternoon, Shea Stadium buzzed with 46,265 fans, a change from their average 1977 attendance of just a few thousand. "It's like the old days," a Met guard said wistfully.

The carnival atmosphere at Shea capped an intense weekend for Tom and Nancy, who had accompanied him to New York. He wished the whole thing were over, becuse he was drained emotionally.

Tom looked forward to seeing his old friends again, but dreaded the emotional wrench of this homecoming. He wondered if his old teammates would still be Buddy, Jerry, and Skip to him, his friends. He hoped they would be more than simply the opposition. To his relief, he discovered no matter what the uniform, Harrelson, Koosman, Grote and Lockwood would always be his buddies.

Once the game began, Tom settled down and managed to put his feelings aside until Bud Harrelson came up to bat. He had never been able to pitch even batting practice to Bud, because he was always afraid he'd hit him. He faltered for a moment when he had to look at Bud for the first time, but then he forced himself to forget who it was and struck him out.

He went on to win a classic 5–1 victory, giving up only six hits and striking out eleven of his former teammates. "It's awfully nice to come home, but that way

Going out to beat the Mets, August 21, 1977

Pitching his 200th victory, September 15, 1977, against the Dodgers

was no fun," he said after the game. "It was too emotional. I was aware they were up there at bat, but I tried to block it out of my mind, and now I'm awfully glad it's over."

As a Met, Tom had been tired in September and had had to push himself to pitch his best, because pitching for a low-scoring team took its toll. But on the Reds, he didn't have that problem. When he joined the team in June, his Met record was 7–3, each victory hard won. He went on to win 14 more games for the Reds, finishing strongly with a 21–6 record that included a league-leading seven shutouts. Also, with his fifth one-hitter on April 17th, he tied a record held by only four other pitchers in National League history.

Goals that were long shots when Tom was a Met

The family at Riverfront Stadium

now were possible. His twentieth victory, which looked remote in May, happened on September 10th, when he pitched a three-hitter against the Braves to win 4–0. It became his fifth season of 20 or more victories. The goal he had set for himself in spring training, winning his 200th game, came on September 15th against the Dodgers. That night he joined Ferguson Jenkins, Gaylord Perry, Kim Kaat and Catfish Hunter as the only active pitchers with 200 or more wins. Now that Tom was a Red, 300 victories, a dream he had given up, returned. "If I can stay healthy and pitch five more years, I should win 300 with this club," he said after his 200th win.

When Tom was traded he hoped the Big Red Machine would once again be World Champions as they had been for two years in a row. But the Reds, even with Tom, couldn't jump the front-running Dodgers. "Seaver wasn't enough," the Dodgers crowed.

But when the season ended, Sparky Anderson reminded the Dodgers that Tom had won a phenomenal 14 of 17 decisions since he had joined the Reds. Anderson was looking ahead to the next year. "The whole club will be involved in turning it around, but Seaver is the basis for my feeling that we definitely will turn it around. We're not going to fall behind right away, because we'll have the big honcho [Seaver] out there. He'll stop it. He won't let it happen."

Tom, listening to his manager's confidence in him, grinned. It was great to know that even the mighty Reds, not just the hapless Mets, needed him. He couldn't wait until the following spring.

Statistics

Year	Club	W-L	ERA	G	GS	GC	IP	H	R	ER	BB	SO
1966	Jacksonville	12-12	3.13	34	32	10	210	184	87	73	66	188
1967	New York	16-13	2.76	35	34	18	251	224	85	77	78	170
1968	New York	16-12	2.20	36	35	14	278	224	73	68	48	205
1969	New York	25- 7	2.21	36	35	18	273	202	75	67	82	208
1970	New York	18-12	2.81	37	36	19	291	230	103	91	83	283
1971	New York	20-10	1.76	36	35	21	286	210	61	56	61	289
1972	New York	21-12	2.92	35	35	13	262	215	92	85	77	249
1973	New York	19-10	2.08	36	36	18	290	219	74	67	64	251
1974	New York	11-11	3.20	32	32	12	236	199	89	84	75	201
1975	New York	22- 9	2.38	36	36	15	280	217	81	74	88	243
1976	New York	14-11	2.59	35	34	13	271	211	83	78	77	235
1977	NY–Cincinnati	21- 6	2.59	33	33	19	261	199	78	75	66	196
Major League Totals		**203-113**	**2.48**	**387**	**381**	**180**	**2979**	**2350**	**894**	**822**	**799**	**2530**

Championship Series

Year	Club	W-L	ERA	G	GS	GC	IP	H	R	ER	BB	SO
1969	New York	1- 0	6.43	1	1	0	7	8	5	5	3	2
1973	New York	1- 1	1.59	2	2	1	17	13	4	3	5	17
Totals		**2- 1**	**3.00**	**3**	**3**	**1**	**24**	**21**	**9**	**8**	**8**	**19**

World Series

Year	Club	W-L	ERA	G	GS	GC	IP	H	R	ER	BB	SO
1969	New York	1- 1	3.00	2	2	1	15	12	5	5	3	9
1973	New York	0- 1	2.40	2	2	0	15	13	4	4	3	18
Totals		**1- 2**	**2.70**	**4**	**4**	**1**	**30**	**25**	**9**	**9**	**6**	**27**

All-Star Games

Year	Club	W-L	ERA	G	GS	GC	IP	H	R	ER	BB	SO
1967	National	0- 0	0.00	1	0	0	1	0	0	0	1	1
1968	National	0- 0	0.00	1	0	0	2	2	0	0	0	5
1969	National			(Selected; did not play)								
1970	National	0- 0	0.00	1	1	0	3	1	0	0	0	4
1971	National			(Selected, did not play)								
1972	National			(Selected; did not play)								
1973	National	0- 0	0.00	1	0	0	1	0	0	0	1	0
1975	National	0- 0	27.00	1	0	0	1	2	3	3	1	2
1976	National	0- 0	4.50	1	0	0	2	2	1	1	0	1
1977	National	0- 0	9.00	1	0	0	2	4	3	2	1	2
Totals		**0- 0**	**4.50**	**7**	**1**	**0**	**12**	**11**	**7**	**6**	**4**	**15**

MAJOR LEAGUE SHUTOUTS: 46
MAJOR LEAGUE ONE-HITTERS: 5

MAJOR LEAGUE HITTING: AB—966, H—138, HR—9, RBI—60, Pct.—143

Index